271

Managing Editor Chris Milsome
Editor Chester Fisher
Design Patrick Frean
Picture Research Ed Harriman
Production Philip Hughes
Illustration John Shackell
　　　　　　Tony Payne
　　　　　　Colin Rose
　　　　　　Janet Munch
　　　　　　Marilyn Day
Maps Matthews & Taylor Associates

Photographic sources Camera Press,
J. Alan Cash Ltd, Central Press Photos,
Martin Chillmaid, Citroen, Christian Dior,
Richard Clapp Photography, Colorific,
Contemporary Films, Coloursport, French
Commisiariat-Général, French Tourist
Office, Giraudon, Food from France,
Keystone, Mary Evans Picture Library,
Popperfoto, Picturepoint, Presse Sports,
Radio Times Hulton Picture Library,
Rex Features, Uniphoto, Roger Viollet,
Frank Whitchurch
Asterix and Lucky Luke cartoons by
permission of Dargoud Editeur

First published 1973
Reprinted 1975, 1976
Macdonald Educational Ltd.
Holywell House, Worship Street,
London E.C.2

© Macdonald Educational Ltd. 1973

ISBN 0 356 04624 9 (cased edition)
ISBN 0 356 05466 7 (limp edition)

Made and printed by
Morrison & Gibb Limited
Edinburgh, Scotland

France

the land and its people

Danielle Lifshitz

Macdonald Educational

Contents

France a cross-roads

Gentle France

The area now known as France has been inhabited by Man for hundreds of thousands of years. Some of the oldest human remains have been found in South-Western France. That it has long been a home for man is not surprising. It is an attractive land, easy to reach, with great natural resources. A land through which people of many races and civilizations have passed and mingled.

In prehistoric times several races made France their home. The Celts, from Central Europe, had made it the centre of their settlement by about 1,000 BC. They called it Gaul. Colonists from Greece founded the port of Marseilles about 600 BC.

The many invasions

The Romans were quick to realize the richness of Gaul. They made it their first province north of the Alps in the first century BC. The Gauls swiftly adapted to Roman civilization during the four centuries of occupation.

The fall of the Roman Empire began a new series of invasions, from Germanic tribes such as the Visigoths, the Burgonds and the Franks. The Franks won and founded the beginning of what was to become France. They ruled for over four centuries but were always fighting invaders from all sides. The Norsemen of Norway and Denmark were one of the strongest and seized the area now known as Normandy. All over France fortresses were built to fend off invaders.

By the 15th century France had almost become the country we know today. Other peoples were to invade or seek France as a refuge but the basic character was formed.

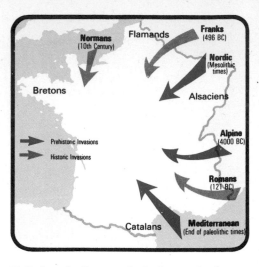

▼ Ruins of a Roman city in the south of France, at Vaison-La-Romain. This part of France is rich in Roman remains such as amphitheatres, arenas and bridges.

▲ Prehistoric cave paintings at Lascaux in south-western France. These horses were painted in Late Palaeolithic times, about 20,000 years ago. The many caves found in this part of France have proved that France was one of the earliest homes of man. The cave art found is said to be among the most beautiful ever discovered.

▶ Menhirs in Brittany. In the Breton language menhir means standing stone. They were probably erected in Neolithic times, about 4,000 B.C. The stones stretch out in long lines and may have been the tombstones of important people.

▲ A piece of the famous Bayeux tapestry which tells the story of the Norman conquest of England by William the Conqueror. The Normans, Scandinavians in origin, invaded France in the tenth century.

▶ A statue of Charlemagne (742-814) who rose from being King of the Franks to become Emperor of most of Western Europe. At his death the Empire crumbled due to numerous invasions.

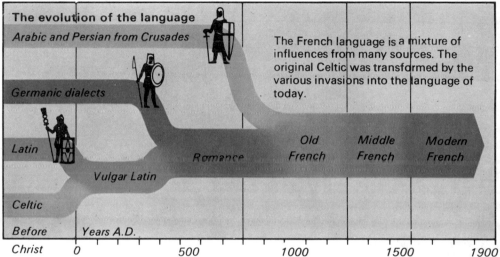

The evolution of the language

Arabic and Persian from Crusades

Germanic dialects

Latin

Celtic

Vulgar Latin

Romance

Old French Middle French Modern French

Before Christ Years A.D. 0 500 1000 1500 1900

The French language is a mixture of influences from many sources. The original Celtic was transformed by the various invasions into the language of today.

▼ The medieval city of Carcassone near the Pyrenees. The strong walls were needed to protect it from attacks by neighbouring lords.

The city commanded many routeways and was vital for defence. Such fortifications preserve the architecture of the time.

The French influence

A leading nation

France is well placed to influence events. She lies at the far western end of Europe surrounded by all the countries who at some time have influenced the fate of the world. France is also the largest of these countries.

Several times in her history France has emerged as a leading nation; in the 13th century when Louis IX led the crusades; in the 17th century under Louis XIV; and at the time of the Revolution and under Napoleon, when France was a major influence upon the politics and ideas of the time.

France today has less political and economic influence than she had; but she still ranks among the "five great powers" and is determined to rank higher still.

A major language

French is the native language of more than 70 million people and is a source of great pride to the French. Strict rules were laid down in the 17th century to prevent its changing. It is, also, still spoken in the former French colonies in Africa and the Far East.

Until recently French was the universal language of diplomats; and was an essential second language of all European aristocrats, and educated men who wanted to read the works of the many great French writers and philosophers.

Cultural prestige

France still commands enormous cultural prestige for her modern artists, architects, writers, philosophers and scientists. She also leads with luxury products such as clothes, perfume and wine.

▲ A French missionary on Lake Chad in 1903. By way of religious missions and armed conquests, France managed to bring its culture very deep into Africa. In many countries, French is still spoken as a first language.

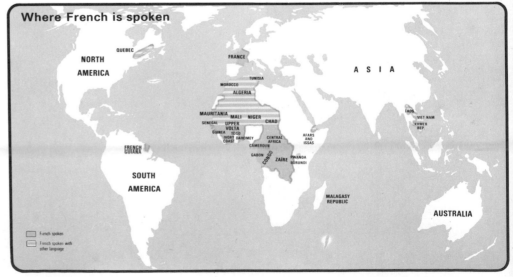

Where French is spoken

NORTH AMERICA
QUEBEC
SOUTH AMERICA
FRANCE
TUNISIA
MOROCCO
ALGERIA
MAURITANIA
SENEGAL
GUINEA
IVORY COAST
UPPER VOLTA
TOGO
DAHOMEY
MALI
NIGER
CHAD
CAMEROUN
CENTRAL AFRICA
GABON
CONGO
ZAÏRE
AFARS AND ISSAS
RWANDA
BURUNDI
FRENCH GUIANA
ASIA
LAOS
VIET NAM
KHMER REP.
MALAGASY REPUBLIC
AUSTRALIA

French spoken
French spoken with other language

▲ The signing of the Vietnam peace treaty on January 4, 1973, in Paris. For hundreds of years Paris has been considered an ideal place for diplomatic conferences and delicate discussions.

▲ Jean-Jacques Rousseau (1712–1778), a world famous thinker and writer. His ideas about society have had an international influence.

Some French gifts to the world

▶ Until recently, French fashion has had a dominating influence on the world. Every season the Parisian couture houses hold shows of new designs. They are eagerly awaited and the best ideas copied around the world.

▶ French cuisine is renowned for its quality and delicacy. The art is not only in the cooking but in the presentation of the dishes and in the choice of wines to accompany the meal.

▲ A painter in Montmartre, one of the most artistic districts of Paris. Since the end of the 19th century, Paris has attracted great artists such as Van Gogh, Picasso, Renoir, Degas. Many painters have based their work on Parisian scenes.

◀ French wines are considered to be the best in the world. France is a large producer and exporter of wines. The biggest customers are Britain and the U.S. Only the best wines are exported.

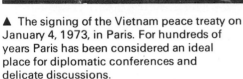

◀ The French language is very subtle and adaptable. For many years it has been considered as the language of diplomacy and also love. Manners are thought to be very important by the French.

The family at home

How the typical family budget is divided

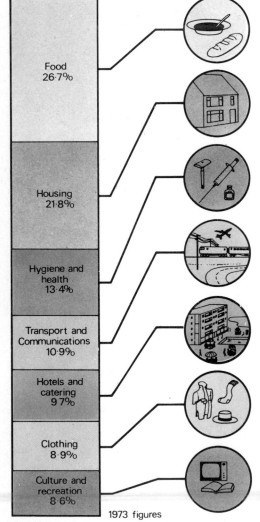

Food 26·7%

Housing 21·8%

Hygiene and health 13·4%

Transport and Communications 10·9%

Hotels and catering 9·7%

Clothing 8·9%

Culture and recreation 8·6%

1973 figures

▶ Another side of French home life. A farm in Normandy, one of the richest agricultural regions. Some villages, especially in poor and mountainous regions, are very remote and do not even have the simplest of modern conveniences.

▲ A street in Nantes lined with apartment buildings. Such streets can be found in any large town throughout France.

▼ A street in Bordeaux. As the majority of French people live in towns and travel to work by car, traffic jams are very frequent.

The private home

The Frenchman sees his home as a retreat from the world. He likes to decorate it in his own style and to use as much originality as possible. He also guards it like a fortress. If he lives in a town, his fortress is usually a flat in an apartment house guarded by the "concièrge" (the porter). This is often a woman of forbidding personality. In the country he will probably have his own house, guarded by a fierce dog.

The changing pattern

The family is an essential part of French life. Parents like to see a lot of their children. They demand much respect but in return they allow them to stay at home until a late age.

In recent years this closeness of family life has begun to change. Many companies now only allow one hour for lunch instead of two and so working parents cannot go home for lunch. Schools now provide lunches and pupils may remain at school. In addition the government is encouraging mothers to go to work by providing day nurseries and schools for children from the age of two.

▲ The house of the family shown below. They live in Valenciennes, an industrial city in Northern France. During the last 20 years, hundreds of thousands of houses and flats have been built to accommodate the growing population and to replace old houses.

▶ A family evening. Family life in recent years has become centred around the television. However, when there is little of interest on television, the family is content to spend the evening playing games or talking.

▲ Mother and children in the kitchen. While the mother is cooking, the children will help to set the table and do the washing-up. French housewives usually cook very simple balanced meals

▲ The lounge. Like many French homes, the furniture is expensive period furniture which is probably rather uncomfortable. However it is not likely to go out of fashion and will be expected to last for life.

▲ The daughter's bedroom. She spends much time in her room, doing her homework, listening to records with friends or reading. It is arranged in a convenient way but is completely to her own taste.

Leisure and pleasure

Finding time to relax

The French are a hard working people. Parents seldom reach home before 7 p.m. and children are given a lot of homework. Evenings are spent watching television, talking, reading, or playing games. Weekends are a chance to get away from town. Some have another house in the country. Others visit friends, go on picnics or enjoy the loneliness of fishing.

When the weekend is spent at home, there is always plenty to do. Father will wash the car and perhaps watch the football match on TV. Children will play with their friends or read their favourite magazines.

The entertainers

The cinema is very popular in France. The French have their own popular stars such as Louis de Funès, Jean Paul Belmondo, Alain Delon, Jeanne Moreau and Yves Montand. France is one of the top five producers of feature films. Many are made specially for the home market and are not usually shown abroad.

In popular music, the French generally prefer ballad-singers such as Georges Brassens and Barbara, though there are many pop-singers.

French radio is operated by the state and has three main networks: France-Inter, France-Culture and France-Musique. There are three television channels, two of which are in colour.

The theatre and classical music have an important place in French life. Many children learn to appreciate these early by visiting theatres and concerts on Wednesdays, which is a day off school.

▲ Fishing is the favourite sport of more than 3½ million Frenchmen. It is relaxing, peaceful, and allows time to think.

▲ Watching sport is the national pastime. In summer the stadiums attract millions of fans.

A typical day on television

Channel I
12.30 **TwelveThirty** a programme of songs. 13.00 **News.** 13.15 **The Young** a film of a weekend in the country. 13.35 programmes close.
16.20 **Programmes for Children** songs, cartoon films, games. 18.30 **To Live in the Present** a film for children about undersea exploration. 18.40 **The Adventures of Colargol the Bear** a story; **The Magic World of Isabelle** a play. 19.20 **Regional News.**
19.45 **News.** 20.15 **Arpad the Tzigan** a series. 20.35 **Medical Research** an appeal for charity.
20.45 **The Big Chess-Board** songs, ballet and interviews with celebrities.
23.30 **News**

Channel II
14.30 **Today Madame** how to protect a baby's health before birth.
15.15 **Daktari** an African adventure series. 16.05 programme close.
19.00 **Figures and Letters** an adult quiz on literature, science and current affairs. 19.20 **Regional News**
19.45 **A time for Living and a Time for Loving** a daily serial 20.00 **News.**
20.35 **Medical Research** an appeal for charity. 20.45 **Songs** with Adamo, Gilbert Becaud, Claude Francois and others. 12.30 programmes close.

Channel III
18.45 **News.** 18.50 **Wild Herbs** a serial. 19.20 **Regional News**
19.40 **Clignotant** a film for the young with Katia Cavagnac and Woody Allen about Buster Keaton. 19.55 **To Live in New York** songs and music of New York. 20.30 **Destinies of this Century** about the Sino-Japanese War and Mao-Tse-Tung 21.25 **A country and a Music** Ireland and memories of its people. 22.20 News.

◄ Playing boules is everybody's pet sport. Each player has two metal balls which he throws in turn. The nearest one to the jack ball wins. A good tactic is to try to knock an opponent's ball away from the jack.

▲ Card playing is very popular, especially in the South, whilst sitting outside a café.

▼ The French are great readers, especially of magazines and newspapers. Most of the publications shown sell over one million copies per issue.

▲ Brigitte Bardot, probably the most famous French film actress.

▲ Alain Delon and Jean Paul Belmondo who are leading film actors.

▲ Barbara, a ballad-singer. She has a very special voice.

▲ Louis de Funès, a very funny film actor. His humour is very French.

How leisure time is spent

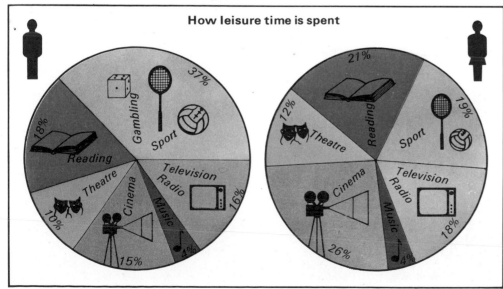

Cafés and restaurants

Eating as an art

One can nearly always find good food anywhere in France for the French put the pleasure of the palate above all others. Gastronomy is as much an art as music or painting.

The restaurant is an important focus of this natural interest in eating. There is a great variety of foods and dishes in France and many restaurants offer one of these as a speciality.

A Parisian may never have been to the Louvre museum but he almost certainly will know of "a marvellous little restaurant, not too expensive, where the snails are 'out of this world' and the Beaujolais is 'Mmm'." With the amount of expert advice available it is unlikely that the stranger will ever have a bad meal!

A meeting place

Equally important is the café on the street corner. Every street corner! One may find good food in a café but French cafés are mainly meeting places not just for eating and drinking.

Every Frenchman has his "own" café where he is known and where he always meets the same people at the same time. Thus cafés act as "clubs" and the membership fee is the price of a cup of coffee and a sandwich.

Cafés stay open from the very early morning till very late at night. One may leave after five minutes or one can play cards, study, read or sit and talk the night away with one's friends. One of the main occupations in a café, however, is sitting quietly watching the world go by!

▲ The waiter is the most important person in the café. He must have a good memory to remember orders.

▶ A painting called L'Absinthe (The Absinthe Drinker) by Degas, a famous French painter of the 1880s. It shows a typical Parisian scene of the time. Poverty and despair are being drunk away in the cafe. Absinthe is a drink made from aniseed and is very powerful.

▲ This is a typical café window as seen from the outside. Even in winter people can sit on the terrace as it is heated. Any drink is available in a café and at any time.

▲ A very famous café in Paris.

► A menu of a Le Routier restaurant. This type of restaurant is found near main roads all over France. They are aimed at lorry drivers but anybody can use them. They serve cheap but good food.

▼ Eating at good restaurants is considered to be one of the great pleasures of life by the French. France has large numbers of excellent restaurants.

Vendredi 18. Juillet

LES ROUTIERS

Au Rendez Vous des Routiers 9 Rue Goncourt Chalonville

MENU
à 16ᶠ.00
Couvert et Service 12% Compris

Hors d'Oeuvre au Choix	Salade de tomates Filets de Hareng Oeuf dur en salade
1 Plat Garni au Choix	Boeuf Gros sel Beafteack pommes frites Poulet Rôti Cresson
1 Fromage ou 1 Dessert au Choix	Camembert, Cantal Compote d'Abricots
1 Boisson au choix	¼ Vin Rouge ou Blanc ¼ Eau Minerale ¼ Bière

▲ The café is a most convenient place to meet friends, discuss business or to spend an evening alone. It is very pleasant in summer to sit out on the terrace.

▲ Many cafés have a television which is watched mainly for sporting events. Many people come to the café just to watch one programme. Each has a public telephone booth.

▲ Cafés displaying the sign "Tabac" are the only places allowed by the authorities to sell cigarettes. They also sell stamps and lottery tickets. Public toilets are also there.

Shops, markets and supermarkets

Looking for the best buy

Food is expensive in France, but the French do not mind spending a large part of their family budget on it. In fact, they always go for the best.

Housewives like to buy simple food, which is healthy and tasty. The family expects to eat meat, vegetables, fruit, cheese, bread and wine every day. They also prefer bottled mineral waters to ordinary water from the tap.

For the best choice and prices there are the local markets, which are held in nearly every village and town. They are open in the mornings, either two days a week or permanently. In the country local people set up stalls and sell their own fruit and vegetables and dairy produce, and many people do their week's shopping there.

Long hours and friendly service

Modern supermarkets are now being built all over France, many of them with large car parks and other conveniences.

But a lot of French people prefer their little local shops to supermarkets. They usually know the man who runs each shop, and can have a chat with him while doing their shopping. He will know what they usually buy, such as the make of wine, and will give them better service than they would get in a supermarket.

Food shops in France are open for very long hours. There are no regulations, but the usual times are from 7 a.m. until 8 p.m. or even later. This enables the working housewife to shop before or after work. By law, shops must close one day a week and for four weeks holiday a year.

▶ A "Boulangerie". France has almost as many bread shops as cafés. Each family buys between one and three long loaves every day. They like to know that the baker makes his own bread and cakes.

▼ A "boucherie" or butcher shop combined with a "charcuterie". Pork meat products are sold by a charcuterie. Meat can be cut to any requirement a customer may have.

French money

▲ A supermarket near Paris. Prices are very low but many French people still prefer the small shops.

▲ An onion stall on the roadside in Normandy. Brittany and Normandy are big producers of onions. Brittany specializes in potatoes.

▶ The main street market in Marseilles on the Avenue du Prado. Fresh fruit, vegetables, meat and fish are sold there every morning Markets also sell cheap clothes and haberdashery.

▼ Some French coins and notes. There are 100 centimes in a franc. One franc is worth about 11 pence.

Eating the French way

ONION SOUP GRATINÉE
(for 3-4 people)
2 tablespoons butter or oil
1 lb. onions, thinly sliced
½ teaspoon salt
1 oz. flour
1½ pints beef or chicken stock
6-8 slices of French bread
1 teaspoon olive oil
1 clove garlic
2 tablespoons grated cheese

QUICHE LORRAINE (for 4-5 people)
Pastry:
6 oz. plain flour
pinch of salt
3 oz. butter
1 oz. lard
a little cold water to mix

Filling:
1 egg and 1 yolk
1 oz. grated cheese
salt and pepper
2½ oz. milk
2 oz. bacon, diced
1 small onion, thinly sliced
½ oz. butter

VINAIGRETTE DRESSING
(for salads or cold vegetables)

2 tablespoons vinegar
5 tablespoons olive or nut oil
1 teaspoon French mustard
a pinch of salt and pepper

Typical meals for a day

Breakfast:
7.30 a.m.   Black or milky coffee or
(weekdays) chocolate. Bread, butter
9.00 a.m.   and jam. Croissants on
(Sundays)   Sundays.

Lunch:
12.30 p.m.   Artichokes vinaigrette,
(weekdays) roast veal with
1.30 p.m.   cauliflower cheese.
(Sundays)   Crème caramel and fruit.

Tea:
4.00 p.m.   Bread and chocolate, or
                   sometimes tea and cakes.

Dinner:
7.30 p.m.   Onion soup,
(weekdays) cold veal or quiche
8.00 p.m.   lorraine, salad,
(Sundays)   cheese and fruit.

Cooking, a traditional skill

In France, cooking is an art, a skill which is passed on from generation to generation. Food is one of the most popular topics of conversation; so much so that other people sometimes wonder whether the French eat in order to live, or live in order to eat!

Even so, people eat far less nowadays than they did in the past. Sophisticated dishes are served in restaurants, but housewives prepare simpler, more healthy meals. Their aim is to draw the most goodness from the food and present it in the most attractive way. For this reason, the French say they can tell a good cook from the way he prepares a simple omelette.

The family meal

The two family meals in France are lunch and dinner. Midday lunch is usually the main meal and dinner a lighter one.

Before the meal, the table is laid with plates, knives and forks, mustard, water, napkins, bread and wine. The long, crusty loaves are served sliced in a basket and eaten with everything except pudding. If there are guests, wines are carefully chosen to match the dishes being served. When the family is alone, they drink the ordinary red wine.

The meal itself can be quite an event. There could be four or five courses, each brought to the table separately. On special occasions, or when there are guests lunch may last for several hours. Afterwards, everyone relaxes with a cup of strong black coffee.

Melt the butter or oil in a heavy saucepan and stir in the onions and salt. Cook on a low heat, stirring occasionally, until the onions are golden brown (about 20 mins.). Sprinkle the flour over the onions, stir and cook for 2-3 mins. Take off the heat and stir in the heated stock. Return the soup to the heat and partly cover with a lid. Simmer for 20-30 mins. Add salt and pepper if necessary.

While the soup is simmering, brush the bread slices with oil and bake, in a medium oven, until lightly browned (about 15 mins. on each side). Rub each slice with a cut clove of garlic.

Pour the soup into a tureen, put the bread slices on top and spread with grated cheese. Sprinkle with melted butter or oil and put under the grill until the cheese is melted and brown.

Sift the flour into a bowl with the salt. Drop in the butter and lard and cut into small pieces with a knife. When they are well covered in flour, mix with your fingertips until the mixture looks like breadcrumbs. Make a well in the centre, add the water, and mix in with a knife. With your fingers, press the mixture into a firm dough, adding more water if necessary. Sprinkle some flour on a wooden board, and knead the dough until smooth. Put in the refrigerator for 30 minutes.

Beat the eggs in a basin, add the cheese, salt and pepper, and milk. Melt the butter in a small pan and cook the bacon and onions until just golden. Add to the egg mixture, and mix.

Butter a 7-inch flan ring or pie tin. Roll out the pastry and line the bottom and sides of the ring or tin. Fill the centre with the egg mixture. Bake in a fairly hot oven (Reg. 5, 370°) for about 30 minutes, or until firm and golden brown. This can be eaten hot or cold.

Put the ingredients in a cup or small bottle and mix or shake well. Add to crisp, washed salad or cold cooked vegetables just before serving.

If you cannot get French mustard, English mustard can be used. You can add a pinch of sugar or fresh, chopped chives to this basic dressing. If you like, put a cut clove of garlic in the dressing, but remember to take it out before serving!

Some famous regional dishes

Tripes à la mode de Caen
▲ This method of cooking tripe is the speciality of Normandy. It is a very old dish, said to have been eaten by William the Conqueror before he set out to defeat the English in 1066. The recipe includes Calvados, the fiery liqueur made from apples, and is traditionally served in this special dish.

Homard à l'armoricaine
▲ The fishermen of Brittany are famous throughout the world for their catches of lobsters. This particular method of cooking lobster takes its name from the ancient name for Brittany, Armor. The sauce for this dish includes tomatoes, garlic, herbs, wine and brandy.

Cassoulet
▲ This is the great speciality of the people of Languedoc, in the south-west of France. It is a stew made from goose or duck, pork or lamb, sausage meat and white beans. The dish was originally introduced to the region by the Roman invaders, nearly 2,000 years ago.

Bouillabaisse
▲ The cooking along the south coast of France is very highly flavoured. This famous dish from the great port of Marseilles is no exception. It is a fish stew which can include as many as 20 different types of Mediterranean fish and shellfish, as well as tomatoes, garlic and onions.

The changing face of France

▶ New flats in Creteil, outside Paris. Many towns are being completely rebuilt. The demand for houses is very urgent and the government has had to build tall cheap houses at great speed.

▼ Old houses in Bayonne. Over two million French people live in houses built between 1750 and 1815. Only a third of the population live in houses with a bath or shower. Only eight out of ten homes have running water.

Concorde, the Franco-British supersonic aircraft, represents the leap forward which France has taken in recent years. Industrial production is booming. If this continues, France is likely to become the richest European country and the third industrial power in the world.

An industrial awakening

France's progress towards industrialisation has been much slower than that of her neighbours. Unlike Britain or Germany, she did not have an industrial revolution in the 19th century. In the past she had great agricultural wealth and a high regard for her prosperous crafts and has been less in need of industry.

Until the 1950s, more people lived in the country than in towns, and even now there are many people living in farms and tiny villages with no modern conveniences.

The migration to the towns

Since World War II, France has been rapidly changing. People are leaving the hard life of the country and moving to towns, where their standard of living will be better.

This has created new problems. Jobs, homes and schools have had to be found for the new town-dwellers, and the state has found it hard to keep pace with the changes.

Whole new towns have been created in the country, and industries have moved there or new ones have been started. Many small towns depend on one industry.

After a slow start, industrial France is now growing fast and may soon outstrip her neighbours. Amongst all these changes, some of the unique character of the country may be lost.

▲ Agriculture as it is still carried out in many parts of France. The peasant farmers are often reluctant to abandon the old ways which have been used for hundreds of years. Many farms are very small and difficult to modernize. Go-ahead farmers are joining together to buy modern equipment such as tractors.

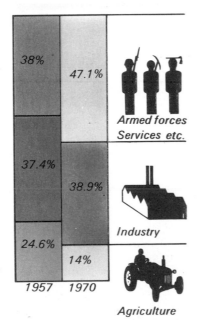

How agriculture is losing ground

	1957	1970	
Armed forces Services etc.	38%	47.1%	
Industry	37.4%	38.9%	
Agriculture	24.6%	14%	

In recent years the proportion of the population engaged in agriculture has rapidly declined. Industry and services such as commerce and construction have steadily gained numbers.

▲ A production line in the Citroën car factory. Between 1965 and 1970, France made approximately 10% of the cars manufactured in the world.

▼ The Pleumeur-Boudou Telecommunications station in Brittany which receives messages relayed by satellites in space.

A land of many contrasts

▶ Fishing boats unloading their catch in the Loire-Atlantique. This region with Vendée and Brittany are the main French fishing areas. They catch 75% of all French fish requirements.

▼ A view of Strasbourg, the beautiful capital of Alsace, on the frontier with Germany. The peoples of Alsace and Lorraine feel very strongly about being considered French as the area has been taken by Germany several times. The Alsacians have an accent and a dialect very close to German.

Specialities and traditions

Although the ancient provinces of France no longer have any administrative power, they are still very important.

Each province has its own history, folklore and customs which have contributed to the country as a whole. The local dialects are still spoken and the costumes worn on special occasions.

Many provinces are renowned for certain specialities, such as wine or cheeses and many are famous for a particular trade.

French men and women have very strong ties with the province from which they come. If they are living in other parts of France, or abroad, they often have gatherings of people from their province.

Parisians sometimes look down on the "provincials", but on the whole the French are very proud of this great heritage.

Things to see in France

Mount St. Michel

Breton Prehistoric remains

Cognac Brandy

Motor rac at Le Man

Lim pott

Oil-refining at Bordeaux

Concorde at Toulouse

A centralized administration

Before the revolution in 1789, France was divided into provinces. These had come about naturally over the years as a result of wars and royal marriages.

Napoleon reorganized the administration of the country and divided it into "departments". There are now 95 departments, each named after the principal river running through it. Every department has an identification number which is used on letters and car number-plates.

At the head of the department is a main town with a Prefect and a smaller town with a Sub-prefect. Each town and village elects a Mayor and a Municipal Council.

The departments themselves are grouped into regions, each administered by a Regional Prefect and a Regional Council. The centre of the administration is in Paris.

Heavy industry

Coal mining

Champagne

Châteaux

Strasbourg Cathedral

Old volcanoes at Le Puy

Perfume at Grasse

Winter sports

boys in Camargue

Côte d'Azur

▲ A view of Argentat in Corrèze. This department is in the Limousin, one of the most beautiful but poorest areas of France.

▼ An aerial view of Fontainebleau near Paris which was built as a royal hunting lodge. It is still surrounded by forest.

Some traditional costumes

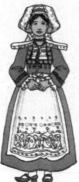

Brittany *Savoy Alps* *Basque* *Brittany*

25

Wine and cheese makers to the world

Expert supervision

The type and quality of a wine depend on a combination of the soil, the amount of sun and the grower's skill.

France is one of the largest exporters of wine in the world, so special precautions are necessary in its manufacture to ensure that quality is maintained.

The viruses and hail-stones are the greatest enemies of the vine. The grower is partly protected by the state, which insures his crops against weather damage. The whole process of wine-making is supervised by experts who taste and approve the wine before it is bottled and sold.

Famous throughout the world

Wine and cheese are products of the French provinces and have a world-wide reputation for excellence. They are extremely important in France as they accompany every meal.

The country produces over 300 different kinds of cheese, and there are over 250 officially registered wines, plus many more unregistered ones.

Differences in climate, soil and manufacture give each product a "personality" of its own. When finished, the wine or cheese takes the name of the village, town or region in which it is made.

Wine bottles come in many shapes

▲ A wine chateau and its vineyard.

▲ Grapes have to be picked at exactly the right time. The wine made will be affected by the type of grape, the soil of the area, the weather and the skill of the grower. Even the best vineyards produce bad wine in some years.

▲ The entire grape is used in the production of wine. Once its skin is broken, the yeast cells react with the sugar to make alcohol. Today most grape crushing is done by machines. The juice obtained is then pumped into vats and left to ferment.

▲ When fermentation is complete, the wine is put into bottles. Some wines such as Beaujolais can be drunk at once but others have to mature in the bottle for several years. Red wine contains about 10% alcohol and white about 11%.

The main wine and cheese products of France

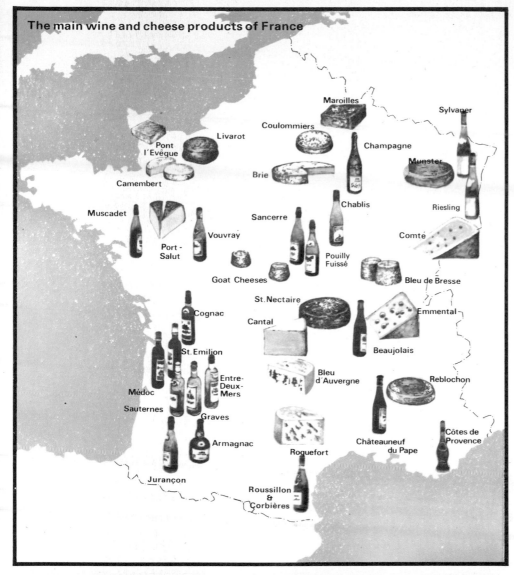

▲ Every region in France supports a large population of milk-giving animals which provide the raw material for cheese. Roquefort cheese is made from ewe's milk. This special type of blue-veined cheese can only be produced in the town of Roquefort in southern France. French law protects this right.

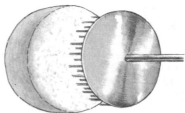

▲ The secret of Roquefort lies not in the actual making of the cheese but in the way it is matured. A powerful mould is injected into the cheese to produce the blue-veined character.

▲ Beneath the town are vast natural caves in which the air is cold and wet. The cheese is left here to mature slowly.

▲ French cheeses are made in a vast number of ways which produce the variety which is without rival. They may be made from cow, ewe or goat milk. The most famous cheeses are matured over long periods, but some, such as cream cheeses, can be eaten quickly. Mature cheeses can be divided into five types: soft-paste (eg Camembert), blue-veined (eg Roquefort), semi-hard (eg Cantal), hard (eg Emmental) and processed.

▲ The caves have the correct conditions to produce the cheese and nowhere else can these be exactly copied. Roquefort cheese is exported to all parts of the world.

27

Paris
the city of light

The heart of France

Paris is the capital of France, and has been its most important town for almost 2,000 years. It was originally founded on two islands on a loop of the river Seine, an accessible and well-protected position.

Paris was in the way of the Roman march through Gaul, and has been even more a cross-roads than France itself.

Today, Paris is the administrative head and the political heart of France. One-sixth of the population lives there and it is a centre of fashion, education and the arts.

Conjuring up the past

To walk through Paris is to walk through the history of France. The 600 year old Notre Dame Cathedral, the Louvre museum, the Place de la Concorde and many other places were the scenes of famous events; and all tell the history of the people and their times.

These old monuments, the lively cafes, the beautiful quays of the Seine and the bright shop windows, all combine to make Paris a most enchanting city.

▼ Montmartre and the church of Sacré-Coeur. Until it attracted artists and poets, Montmartre was a peaceful village on the borders of Paris. Even today old windmills survive. It is an area of narrow streets, stairs and shadows with a good view of Paris. Today it is the centre of Parisian night life with many clubs and restaurants.

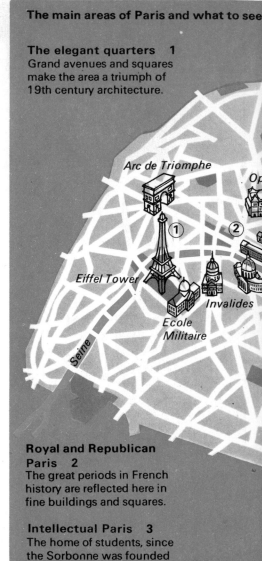

The main areas of Paris and what to see

The elegant quarters 1
Grand avenues and squares make the area a triumph of 19th century architecture.

Arc de Triomphe

Eiffel Tower

Invalides

Ecole Militaire

Seine

Royal and Republican Paris 2
The great periods in French history are reflected here in fine buildings and squares.

Intellectual Paris 3
The home of students, since the Sorbonne was founded in 1250, and recently artists.

▲ A café on the Champs Elysées with the Arc de Triomphe, built by Napoleon, behind.

28

Paris of the night 4
Once the artistic centre, now the focus of Paris night-life.

The cradle of Paris 5
In 300 B.C. Paris was founded on two islands in the Seine. Much early history is here.

Business Paris 6
Trade, from small workshops to the Stock Exchange.

▲ A view of Paris showing how the new Paris lives close to the old Paris. New flats and offices are constantly being built. Some people like these developments but many believe they are disfiguring the old and beautiful areas.

The building of the Eiffel Tower

1. October 8, 1887. Four iron stumps rise from the Champs de Mars, a former military manoeuvre ground. The tower is being built for the Great Exhibition of 1889 by Gustave Eiffel, an engineer. It will be the world's tallest building.

2. June 14, 1888. The first storey of 186 feet (57 m.) is complete. When finished it will have 12,000 parts and will have used 6,000 tons of steel.

3. February 14, 1889. It is almost at its full height of 985 feet (300 m.). The Tower was to become the most famous landmark and symbol of Paris. Today besides being a tourist attraction it is also used for tele-communications.

1

2

3

The fashion magicians

French elegance

Fashion is one of France's most famous exports, and French women are well-known for their simple but elegant way of dressing. All over the western world, women who admire this elegance follow the fashions of the Paris couturiers (dress designers).

Top fashion houses, such as Balenciaga, Cardin, Courrèges and Dior, show seasonal collections. They sell original models of their designs to a small clientele of very rich women.

In recent years, ideas have changed. Many top designers are starting to design for the big clothing manufacturers. These designs will be sold "off the peg" at cheaper prices all over the world. Far more people will be able to dress like the elegant French.

▲ The design of each season's collection is the art of the Grand Couturier. He gives his own style to his creations which are registered and cannot be copied. The models are showing Christian Dior creations.

▲ The sketches are the first stage in designing a collection. These will be used to produce the finished dress.

◄ Some French fashion magazines. They give details about the latest fashions. French women like to be in fashion but always prefer to retain an elegance in dress.

▲ Each season, the couturiers will present a show of their designs for the next season. The designs are kept secret until then to prevent anyone stealing the ideas.

How perfume is made

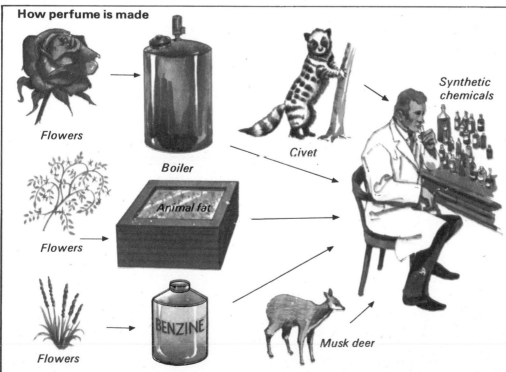

Flowers

Boiler

Animal fat

Flowers

BENZINE

Flowers

Civet

Synthetic chemicals

Musk deer

Most French perfumes are made in the city of Grasse in Provence. Each perfume has a secret formula which is a mixture of many different ingredients. There are several different ways of making perfume. In the oldest method, flowers are boiled up and the oils drawn off. The most pure oil is known as essence. 500 lbs. (226 kg.) of rose flowers are needed to make 1 lb. (0·4 kg.) of rose essence. Another method is to paint a glass plate with animal fat and allow the fat to absorb the perfume from flowers. The perfume is then washed out and the fat made into soap. The third process uses the chemical benzine to extract the essence.

Each perfume is a mixture of essences and also needs substances such as civet and musk (from animal glands) to fix the perfume and stop evaporation. Synthetic chemicals are also used as natural ones are very expensive.

Louis XIV the Sun King

▲ Louis XIV in magnificent ceremonial robes. His clothes were part of his status and brilliance.

▼ The magnificent Palace of Versailles, near Paris, in which Louis established his Court. An army of 36,000 workmen laboured over it for many years.

The beginning of an era

Louis XIV reigned for 68 years, the longest reign in European history. He became king at the age of five in 1643 and began to govern himself at the age of 23. He inherited a kingdom made strong by Cardinal de Richelieu, his father's brilliant prime minister.

A divine right to rule

Louis believed that he was chosen by God to be king, and he centred all government in himself. In his early years, he enlarged France and made her richer. His court was magnificent and produced many artists.

But Louis moved the court from Paris and built a splendid palace at Versailles, 18 miles away. To stop the nobles becoming too powerful, he made them leave their estates and live at court. The country began to suffer because of costly wars and very heavy taxation. Life was hard and the people were very poor.

At the end of his reign, Louis involved France in continual wars. These, and the court's extravagance, ruined the country. When Louis died, in 1715, France was in a poor financial state. He advised his great grandson and successor, Louis XV, not to follow his example.

▲ The King rewarding his officers with the Order of St Louis (created by Louis IX). By giving such honours Louis XIV was attempting to keep his normally rebellious nobles under his domination.

▶ A scene from the siege of Valenciennes in 1677 by Louis XIV. Louis involved France in many wars which were finally ruinous to the country. He insisted that warfare be disciplined and employed great military engineers to plan battles and sieges very carefully.

Molière—a great playwright

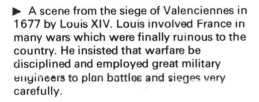

▲ A scene from *Le Bourgeois Gentilhomme* by Molière (*Left*) who is the most famous French dramatist. His work was subsidized by Louis XIV. His plays range from light-hearted farce to violent criticisms of the society of the time. Besides writing plays he was also a leading actor. The French National Theatre, The Comedie Francaise is called Molière's theatre.

▲ The magnificent life of the King, nobles and Church was at the expense of the peasants. This cartoon at the time of the 1789 revolution illustrates the crippling weight of taxation.

Napoleon the little Corsican

A man of destiny

Napoleon Bonaparte was born in Corsica in 1769, the year after it became French territory. He was the second of a family of eight children. His family, though noble, was poor and he needed a financial grant to be educated at a military school in Paris. When the Revolution began in 1789 Napoleon was 20 years of age. He was at once sympathetic to the aims of the Revolution and began to show his great talents.

By 1797, he had already proved his military genius against the Austrian and British armies. The expedition to Egypt, in 1799, made him a national hero. Napoleon was adored by his "Great Army" and by his brilliant oration knew how to inflame their pride and nationalism. He was a tireless worker but strongly believed that his "star" or destiny was leading him to great things.

Emperor of France

At this time France was in confusion as the revolutionary leaders such as Danton, Robespierre and Marat were quarrelling among themselves. A new strong leader was needed. On November 9, 1799, Napoleon was elected First Consul of the French Republic. Within two years he brought peace inside and outside France. He also established constitutional rights and a Code of Law which are still used in France.

In 1804, at the height of his glory, he crowned himself Emperor Napoleon I. His ambition was boundless. He went from victory to victory, except for defeats at sea by Nelson, and dominated the whole of Europe.

The countries of Europe however began to unite against Napoleon. His attempt to conquer Russia in 1812 proved disastrous. In 1813 the combined armies of Europe heavily defeated him and he abdicated in 1814. Though he escaped from exile in 1815 he was quickly defeated at Waterloo. He died alone in exile on the island of St Helena in 1821.

▲ A painting of the execution of King Louis XVI in 1793 during the French Revolution. This event was meant to give full political power to the people. A republic was formed which began a series of reforms. Napoleon began his rise to power at this time.

◄ Napoleon at the battle of Lodi in 1796. This battle in Italy, against the Austrians, and his whole Italian campaign were to reveal his military genius. The treaty which followed assured his fame as a conqueror and a peacemaker in the tradition of the Revolution.

▼ The Napoleonic Empire in 1810. At this time Napoleon was at the height of his power. In 1812 he set out to conquer Russia and his fortunes began to decline.

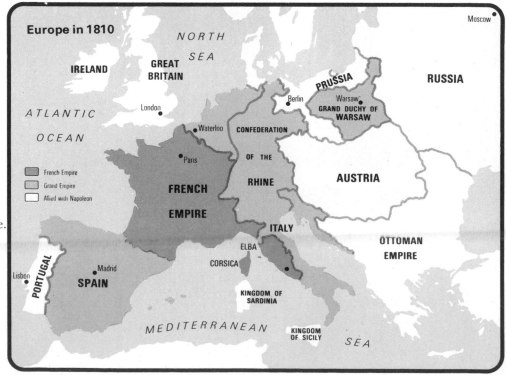

Europe in 1810

The Battle of Aboukir in Egypt in 1798. Though Napoleon won the battle, his fleet was to be destroyed soon afterwards by Nelson at the Battle of the Nile.

▲ Napoleon in his coronation robes after crowning himself Emperor in Notre-Dame Cathedral in 1804. By doing so he revived memories of the Roman Empire.

▲ Napoleon and his wife Josephine. He married her in 1796 and they were divorced in 1809. They had a violent but deep relationship. Napoleon was to marry again.

▲ After his defeat at Waterloo in 1815, Napoleon was immediately exiled to the distant British island of St. Helena. He died there in 1821.

Charles de Gaulle a great leader

Fighting the invaders

Charles de Gaulle was born in 1890. Almost 30 years of French history were to be dominated by his outstanding personality. He trained as a soldier and had risen to high rank when the Germans invaded in 1940.

With the invasion the French government moved south and eventually made its capital at Vichy with Marshal Pétain as Head of State. The Vichy government ruled with the consent of the Germans. Many Frenchmen disagreed with this and either joined the underground resistance movement or, as General de Gaulle did, escaped to Britain. He placed himself at the head of the "Free French" forces and was very involved in the final liberation of France in 1944. After the war, de Gaulle was for a few months President but he resigned and remained in the background for several years.

▲ De Gaulle as a child. He was the son of a headmaster of a Jesuit school and received a very strict education.

▲ De Gaulle leaving Downing Street after the historic broadcast of 1940 encouraging the French not to accept the fall of France as definite. He became the leader of the Free French against the Germans.

▶ Churchill and De Gaulle reviewing French troops in Alsace-Lorraine in winter 1944. After the Normandy landings of June 1944 the allies swept through France and forced the Germans back to their own borders.

◄ Like many great politicians, General De Gaulle was a great orator. Some of his speeches and sayings are still remembered. When he gave a speech, he liked to punctuate it with vast movements of the arms.

▶ A cartoon about De Gaulle which looks at his great ambitions for France and his attempts to dictate to other countries.

President of France

In 1958 General de Gaulle was called upon to stabilize the government and to deal with the Algerian war of independence. He created the Fifth Republic with himself as President. The new constitution gave parliament and ministers less power but the President more power. He ended the Algerian war granting independence to Algeria in 1962.

As President, de Gaulle tried to make France more influential in the world and to build up its economic wealth. However by 1968 his ideas were becoming unpopular and demonstrations throughout France forced him to retire in 1969. He died a year later.

▼ In May and June 1968, there were riots and demonstrations against the De Gaulle Government. One year later, a referendum held said "No" to De Gaulle's future plans.

▲ President De Gaulle and George Pompidou when Prime Minister. Pompidou became President in 1969 and was considered by De Gaulle to be his heir.

▲ This drawing of De Gaulle done in a street in Paris during the events of May 1968 uses a famous saying of his, "I understand you".

▲ The country home of De Gaulle in Colombey-les-deux-Eglises where he lived when not in power.

The school tradition and reform

▲ A modern French school with pupils in the playground before the start of lessons. Many schools are however housed in very old buildings.

State-controlled education

In France, school is compulsory between the ages of 6 and 16. All education is controlled by the state and most schools are free and non-religious. But there are many private schools run on a religious basis where fees are paid.

A good education is considered important, and French parents encourage their children to work hard. School hours are long and there is a lot of homework to do in the evenings. Although one midweek day is free, Saturday morning is school time, so there is not much break for the weekend.

Most people go home for lunch, but there are some pupils who have lunch at school, and some who live in completely. In big towns boys and girls may go to separate schools from the age of 6 onwards, but in small village schools everyone works together. Nobody has to wear uniform.

A changing system

It is not necessary to go to school until the age of 6, but some children go to kindergarten as early as 2 years old. This is a happy time, where one plays games, paints, sings and makes friends.

Primary school lasts for five years and then, between the ages of 11 and 16, students go to a secondary school. At the end of seven years some take the final examination, the baccalauréat, with which they can go to a university or a "grande école".

Secondary schools and universities in France are changing fast because much of the system is very old-fashioned. The number of people in secondary schools has doubled in the last fifteen years, so there are not enough schools or teachers to go round. Many improvements have been planned to keep the standard of education as high as it has been in the past and yet adapt to modern needs.

▲ A typical French classroom. A major problem in schools is overcrowding. There are usually 40 to 50 per class.

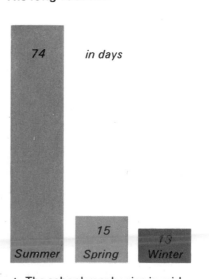

The long vacation

74   *in days*

15   13

Summer   Spring   Winter

▲ The school year begins in mid-September after a very long summer vacation. As can be seen from the diagram other holidays are short compared with the one in summer. There are also brief breaks in the middle of each term.

The French school system

Universities and ''Grande Ecoles''. Students have a choice between arts, law, economics, sciences, medicine or specialized studies. Standards are high.

Vocational training. A further one or two years can be spent in learning about a specialized profession which requires a detailed study.

Apprenticeship or on-the-job training. Skilled and non-skilled workers can undergo this training. Promotion will come with experience.

Lycée or grammar school. The brightest pupils will remain here until 18 and take a classical or a technical Baccalauréat examination.

Short technical school. Pupils may leave here at 16 or go on for a further year and obtain a diploma. They get general and vocational education.

Vocational school. All pupils in this school leave at age 16. They work for a certificate of aptitude in a certain skill or trade.

France has a strictly controlled system of education. The chart gives a simplified summary of the present system. Though there are both private and state schools, the same subjects and courses are offered in both. After primary school pupils enter schools which suit their ability. Some will leave at the age of 16 while others will continue to 18. Some will go to university or take vocational training.

Primary school. This is compulsory from age 6 and pupils learn how to read, write and count. Here they will begin to be graded as regards ability.

Infant school. Though this early school is not compulsory more children are attending. They learn basic skills such as counting and reading.

How time is spent in school

	MONDAY	TUESDAY	WEDNESDAY	THURSDAY	FRIDAY	SATURDAY
8	French	Science	—	Maths	English	
9	Maths or French	Science	—	History or Geography	French	
10	English	German	—	Games	Civics	History or Geography
11	Maths	Gym	—	or Swimming		Art
12	L U N C H					
2	Gym	English	—	French	German	
3	History or Geography	French	—	German	French	
4			—	Maths		

▲ The timetable shows the week of a pupil in the 3rd grade (14 years of age).

All lessons last an hour. One day per week is free.

▲ In the gymnasium. Sport is growing in importance in schools. Until recently, most schools have been poorly equipped with facilities for sport.

Sports and sportsmen

A growing interest

Until recently the French were not a keen sporting nation. Today the situation is quite different. Amateur sport is very popular and French sportsmen are winning major competitions abroad. Many stadiums, swimming pools and other facilities have been built to encourage interest in sport.

The major attractions

The event arousing the most enthusiasm is the Tour de France cycle race. Every evening during the 25 day race, fans watch the arrival of cyclists on television in cafés and shop windows. For several years French cyclists dominated this very tough race. All along the route the competitors find long rows of supporters.

The Le Mans 24 hours car race is also an event which raises national interest. Only the world's best drivers and cars are able to compete in this gruelling race which runs right through a day and a night.

Horse racing is the only sport in which betting is legal and therefore it is very popular. Every Sunday millions wait for the names of the three winning horses to be announced and hope that they have won on the "Tiercé".

Football, rugby, athletics, gymnastics, horse-riding, skiing and swimming are some other popular sports. Olympic champions like Jean-Claude Killy have inspired others to take part in the now very popular sport of skiing.

Less energetic but equally popular with young and old is boules or "Petanque". The game is played anywhere in the open air and is a form of bowls.

▲ Riders in the Tour de France. In the foreground is Raymond Poulidor, one of the most popular French cyclists. All along the route of the Tour, spectators encourage the riders and offer drinks or buckets of water.

The Tour de France
The most popular event in French sporting life is the Tour de France. It takes place every year in July. The first race was in 1903. An average of 150 riders tackle the tortuous 3,000 mile (4,800 km.) course around the perimeter of France. The course changes each year but it always goes through the heat of the South and over 7,000 feet (2,134 m.) mountain passes. Behind the riders trails a vast column of managers, masseurs, reporters, and travelling exhibitions advertising various products. The race has become a very important commercial event and every rider advertises something.

The most successful rider in recent years has been a Frenchman, Jacques Anquetil, who won in 1957, 1961, 1962, 1963 and 1964. He also holds the record for the fastest average time, 23 m.p.h. (37 k.p.h.).

▲ Competitive skiing. Much encouragement and financial support is put into the training of competitive skiers. National and international competitions are very popular.

◀ The Le Mans 24 hours Race is the source of much interest in France. Here, two Porsches race past the grandstand. The most powerful cars and the best drivers in the world take part in this exhausting race.

▼ A race at the famous Longchamps course in Paris. Besides being the opportunity for an elegant fashionable gathering, much betting is done. France has produced some of the most famous horses and jockeys in recent years.

▲ Jacques Anquetil, five times winner of the Tour de France.

▲ Spanghero, one of the most popular French rugby players and captain of the French team

▲ Yves Saint Martin, a very successful jockey who has won many major races.

▲ Jean-Claude Killy, an Olympic gold medallist and winner of the World Cup for skiing.

Holidays
the great exodus

▲ The most popular holiday resorts in France. In summer the coasts are the first choice. The mountain regions are also visited for health reasons. There are many places of historic and artistic interest which get lots of visitors.

The big shutdown

For eleven months of the year, the French think about the twelfth month, when they will take their annual holidays.

Some people like skiing and go on holiday in the winter, but most prefer the summer months. August is the big holiday time, and many large companies close down for the whole month. In the big cities, and especially in Paris, all the theatres and shops close, and the place is deserted except for tourists.

Holiday-makers travel by car or train to camping sites, hotels, rented houses or to stay with relations.

▶ A winter holiday resort called La Ceusaz. In the last ten years, skiing has become very popular. School holidays are the most crowded times but many people also spend weekends in the mountains.

A country of great variety

Most French people are quite satisfied with what their country has to offer and have no wish to travel abroad. Mountains and rivers, sandy beaches and beautiful countryside are all available in France.

French schools break up for two and a half months of summer holiday on July 1. While their parents are working, the children may stay with relatives in the country or go to a holiday colony (colonie de vacances).

These holiday colonies are often organised by the companies in which the parents work. They take place in converted castles and are very cheap, so that as many people as possible can go to them. Each colony is run by 10 leaders and there are normally about 100 children of all ages.

For young and old people who want to travel abroad there are organizations such as the "Club Méditerranée" who own holiday villages in beautiful sites all around the Mediterranean.

Where holidays are spent

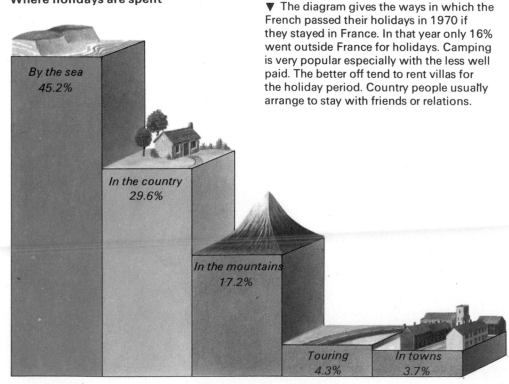

By the sea
45.2%

In the country
29.6%

In the mountains
17.2%

Touring
4.3%

In towns
3.7%

▼ The diagram gives the ways in which the French passed their holidays in 1970 if they stayed in France. In that year only 16% went outside France for holidays. Camping is very popular especially with the less well paid. The better off tend to rent villas for the holiday period. Country people usually arrange to stay with friends or relations.

▲ French people take their annual summer holidays either on July 1 or August 1. Millions of people leave the large towns and rush by car and train to all parts of France. In August Paris is almost deserted except for tourists.

◄ A beach at Ste Maxime on the French Riviera, at the height of summer. Finding a place to sit is likely to waste precious sunshine! The idea is to go back to the office in September with a beautiful tan and a healthy look.

▲ A colonie de vacances. Parents who cannot go on holiday may send their children here. They are very strictly organized. Trained organizers keep the children happy and amused throughout the day. They are strictly controlled by local authorities and are quite cheap.

Getting about in France

Scenes of confusion

The French use their cars a great deal, and traffic jams are frequent and very noisy. Drivers pass the time by hurling insults at one another! The confusion is added to by the many motorcycles on the road. Many of these are driven by children and students, who cannot get a driving licence until the age of 18.

French towns with more than 50,000 inhabitants have several bus routes and sometime even tramways, but only Paris has an underground. The "Metro" was built between 1900 and 1930, and is constantly being extended into the suburbs.

A giant spider's web

The road and railway networks in France are like a huge spider's web, with Paris in the centre. France was a late developer with motorways, but is catching up fast, and roads are being built from east to west and north to south.

The S.N.C.F. (National Society of French Railways) is nearly all electric and quite advanced. It is now introducing turbotrains and aerotrains. The French like to think that their trains are amongst the most punctual in the world.

Air France is an international airline which carries millions of passengers a year, both abroad and within France. To cope with this traffic a third Paris airport is being built. It will be ready in 1975 and will be one of the largest in Europe.

The types of French car

Citroën 15

The French car has always had a character of its own. It is very recognizeable and suits the French character. Most Frenchmen prefer to buy a French car rather than an imported one. Today several companies dominate the market, the most important being Renault and Citröen.

Renault 16

▲ Nice station and local passenger trains. France has a comprehensive and efficient system of railways. The system was largely rebuilt due to war damage. Express trains such as the famous *Mistral* reach an average speed of 84 m.p.h. (135 km.p.h.) on long runs. This express covers the 195 miles (320 km.) from Paris to Dijon in 2 hours 20 minutes and does the 536 miles (863 km.) to Marseilles in 6 hours 40 minutes with only four stops. The *Capitole* which runs from Paris to Toulouse has reached 125 m.p.h. (200 km.p.h.) on a certain stretch. Trains are all electric or diesel.

The Paris metro

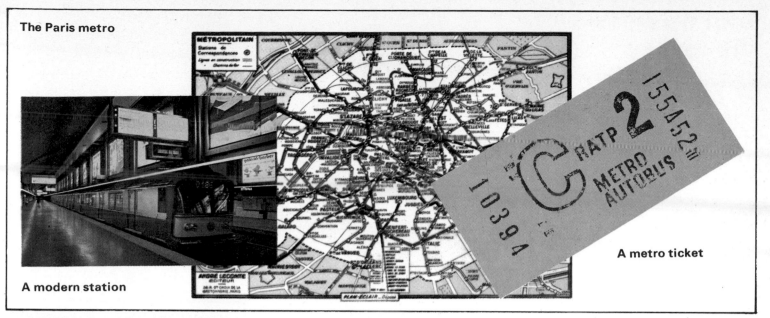

A modern station

A metro ticket

The production of French cars

► The French car industry was founded in 1895, and now ranks third in the world in terms of production. Improvements in technological skills have enabled the industry to produce over three million vehicles per year. Of the four main car producers in France (right), Renault was nationalised in 1946.

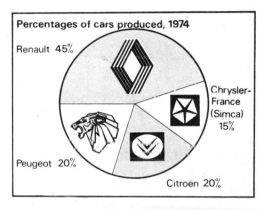

Percentages of cars produced, 1974

Renault 45%

Chrysler-France (Simca) 15%

Peugeot 20%

Citroën 20%

▲ One of the "routes nationales" in France. Most of these roads are lined with trees and have been the cause of many serious accidents. New motorways or "Autoroutes" are replacing these old, narrow roads.

▲ The small motor bicycle or "mobylette" is one of the most popular means of French transport. Young and old choose it for its convenience especially in heavy traffic and for its cheapness.

▲ Bus services are an essential means of transport especially in towns. This shows a Paris bus with the old-fashioned open back.

Invention and discovery

Marie Curie and her husband Pierre made scientific history in 1895 by extracting radium, which gives off radioactivity, from pitchblende. This startling discovery gained them the Nobel prize for physics in 1903. Radium has since been used in numerous ways, especially in medicine.

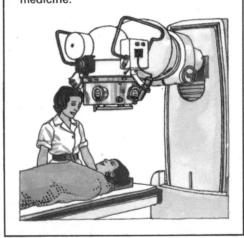

The canal builder

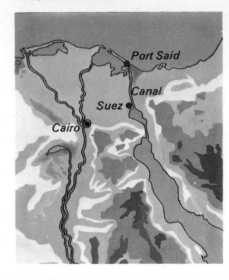

Using hot air

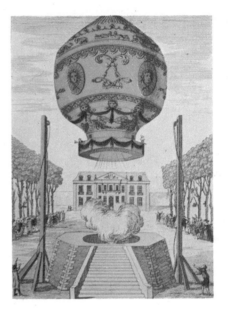

Two brothers, Joseph (Below) and Etienne Montgolfier, were the first to construct a practical hot-air balloon. The first successful flight in 1782 took them six miles (9·6 km.).

First to fly the Channel

▼ Louis Blériot (1872-1936) was the first man to fly long distance. On July 25, 1909, he crossed the English Channel from Calais to Dover in 1 hour 37 minutes. His plane, the Blériot XI, arrived safely except for losing a wheel on landing. He was already a famous figure before this flight, having invented a new type of light for the motor car. Several heavier-than-air monoplanes were designed by Blériot but all crashed. After his historic flight he continued building aircraft and lived to see the development of commercial passenger services.

Blériot XI

▲ Viscount Ferdinand de Lesseps (1805–1894). The French engineer who conceived and built the canal in 1869 across the Isthmus of Suez. This feat changed the economical face of the Western world by cutting the time taken for ships to reach the East.

A father of chemistry

Antoine Lavoisier (1743-94) was the first to discover that burning is a form of chemical reaction. He invented the word "oxygen" and explained why it is so important in the burning process. He was able to obtain pure oxygen in his experiments (Right). He found out that oxygen and nitrogen are major parts of the air. He was beheaded during the Revolution.

Cousteau exploring the depths

Commander Jacques-Yves Cousteau is known world-wide for his exciting discoveries beneath the oceans. After graduating as an officer, he began a career in oceanographic research. He is the inventor of the aqualung, the diving saucer Denise (Right) and an undersea laboratory. By making films and writing books on the exploration of the sea, he has done more than any man alive to popularize the subject.

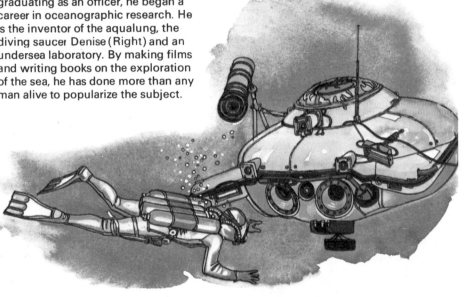

Making moving pictures

Two pioneers of the early cinema were the brothers Louis and Auguste Lumière. Louis was a chemist who from an early age was interested in improving the photograph. By careful work he invented the processes which led to the making of moving film. Working together, the two brothers then invented the cinematograph, an early film projector. Their first film, about factory workers, was made in 1895.

Fighting germs

▶ Louis Pasteur (1822–1895). His discovery in 1847 of microscopic fermentation of germs led him to the science of bacteriology and infectious diseases. He then discovered their prevention by means of immunology and vaccination. Probably his most famous discovery was how to protect man from the bite of an animal with rabies. His researches have transformed medicine, chemistry and everyday life.

Heroes of legend and fiction

The many characters

The French have a huge variety of heroes both in legend and fiction. A boy or girl is likely to encounter innumerable characters, historical, legendary or fictional. Many of these will be international, such as Batman, Robin Hood or Snoopy, but many will be French heroes not always well known abroad.

Some, such as D'Artagnan, Captain Nemo, Guignol and Quasimodo have been on the scene for generations. Others, like Asterix the Gaul and Lucky Luke are fairly new. Asterix is the most popular character amongst both children and adults.

The two most famous writers of adventure stories are Alexandre Dumas and Jules Verne. Dumas wrote about 300 books, all very loosely based on historical events. He was the author of *The Three Musketeers* and *The Count of Monte Cristo*. Jules Verne specialized in scientific adventure stories and many of his predictions have come true. Best known are *Twenty Thousand Leagues Under the Sea* and *Around the World in Eighty Days*.

▲ A scene from *Twenty Thousand Leagues under the Sea*, a novel written by Jules Verne. The hero, Captain Nemo (Nemo in Latin means nobody), has a series of adventures in his submarine *Nautilus*. As the book was written in 1870 it is remarkable for its description of undersea exploration.

◄ D'Artagnan and the Musketeers battling with soldiers sent by the scheming Cardinal de Richelieu. Written in 1844 by Alexandre Dumas as a newspaper serial, the novel, *The Three Musketeers,* is set in 17th century France. The heroes see and prevent many historical tragedies.

▼ Astérix the Gaul, a brave little warrior who refuses to surrender to the Roman conquerors. He and his friend Obélix caricature what the French prefer in themselves.

▲ Guignol, the hero of the French puppet theatre, was created in Lyons in 1795. He is a policeman and only has misadventures.

▲ Lucky Luke, the hero of a comic strip western, by the same authors as Astérix.

▲ The Man in the Iron Mask in the Bastille prison. In a novel by Alexandre Dumas he was the twin brother of Louis XIV and the mask was to prevent him being recognized. He was a real person and spent 40 years there, but his real identity is unknown.

▼ Quasimodo, from Victor Hugo's *Hunchback of Notre-Dame*. He saves the beautiful Esmeralda from being burnt as a witch. Quasimodo was a bell-ringer at Notre-Dame Cathedral and lived among the bells.

▲ The cunning fox from La Fontaine's fable. The crow is flattered and drops the cheese.

Custom and superstition

Some French customs

▲ The French are not gentlemen at the wheel. They love insulting each other.

▲ A policeman will always salute you before fining you.

▲ Kissing one's friends and relations several times is usual.

▲ "After you!" "No, please, after you!" "No, after you." The French are civilized.

Religion and tradition

The French have inherited a vast number of ancient customs and superstitions from the many races and cultures of which they are a mixture. France is a Catholic country and many traditions have acquired a religious significance. Each region has special celebrations, sayings and customs. The national traditions are also carried out in different ways in the regions of France.

Some special days

On Shrove Tuesday, children all over France wear masks or fancy clothes and mothers make pancakes. In Nice there is a Carnival in which a dummy figure is borne through the streets and burnt in the evening on a bonfire. In the Basque Country there is dancing and traditional pantomimes.

Christmas in Provence is more colourful than anywhere else in France. Everybody dresses as shepherds and walks in procession to the churches accompanied by flutes and drums. In the churches are beautiful cribs which have marvellously painted clay figures of the nativity characters. A special meal with fish is then served in every home.

In Brittany, on St. John's Day, the fishermen and their families walk down to the sea carrying crosses to bless their boats and the waters on which they sail.

Manners and sayings

Many different styles and customs have been adopted by the French in their everyday life. Good manners are considered an important part of life and children are taught them from an early age. The language is also rich in sayings and superstitions. Many are international, such as a broken mirror bringing bad luck, while others are peculiar to France.

▲ Seeing a spider in the evening brings hope. In the morning it brings sorrow.

▲ A wedding in Normandy. After leaving the church, the family and guests walk in a procession through the town to the restaurant where the reception is to be held.

► Cars blowing their horns in the Champs Elysées in Paris on December 31 at midnight. Drivers thus wish one another and the whole of France a happy New Year. Special permission is given for this as horn-blowing is usually forbidden.

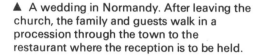

▲ Putting your left foot in it by accident is said to bring you luck.

▲ On May 1 every year, friends and relations give one another bunches of lilies of the valley. This is supposed to bring luck and happiness.

► Fireworks and the Place de La Concorde, Paris, on July 14, the day which celebrates the fall of the Bastille prison during the Revolution. There are dances and fireworks all over France.

◄ The Mardi Gras carnival in Nice on Shrove Tuesday. Floats covered with flowers are taken through the town.

How the French see themselves

Better than the others

The French are a nation of individualists. Everyone considers himself either different or better than others. As a nation they are sure of their superiority over other nations. French products, such as food, trains and post-offices, are thought the best in the world. There is very little attempt to test these ideas as it is assumed that they know what happens abroad. Nothing on earth can be compared with French life according to the typical Frenchman.

However, an enormous amount of energy is spent in protesting and complaining. The French will protest against anything and everybody. It is not that they want things to change. The principle is the most important thing and a need to show that one is important and cannot be tricked.

Emotion and caution

Though the Frenchman usually proceeds with caution, he is also likely to become very excited. A good example is French drivers who have become famous for their heated arguments with each other. In other ways the Frenchman examines things with logic and reason. Some of the greatest philosophers have been French.

Every Frenchman likes to believe that he has got good taste in all aspects of life from food to art. He is also distrustful of innovation and will be slow to accept it. However most Frenchmen dream of inventing a fantastic new thing in some field.

Argument and wit

The pet hate of the Frenchman and the subject of many jokes is the local tax inspector. Cheating the inspector is a favourite pastime and a source of great personal pride. The ability to avoid unpleasant things has grown into a kind of philosophy called the "System D". The term is almost untranslatable but roughly means the ability to get things done cheaply, quickly or better.

Discussions with friends or relations over a meal or a drink are considered great pleasures. People are ready to discuss any subject, but particularly food and politics, simply for the enjoyment it gives. Political discussions nearly always end in violent arguments. Being brilliant and witty in conversation are highly prized qualities. To win an argument, the opponent must be made to look silly or ridiculous.

Some characteristics of the French

▲ The French have a strong sense of the ridiculous. They will not lose an opportunity to make others aware of how ridiculous they appear.

▲ The French do not like to be told what to do. They are very fond of order but do not like authority. They admire discipline as long as it is for someone else.

▲ Culture and wit are the most prized qualities of the man in society. One has to display one's knowledge at any price. Intellect is highly regarded.

▲ Inventing a new machine is the dream of every Frenchman. Being skilled with one's hands while using one's brains is considered a great asset.

▲ An example of the famous "System D" which roughly means to be resourceful and get things done by cutting corners. Special delight comes from avoiding taxation.

▲ The Frenchman puts food and his stomach before most other things in life. He is very particular about what he eats and will go miles for a good meal.

▼ Strolling around the streets without any particular purpose is a popular form of leisure for many French people, especially on Sundays.

▲ Jean Yanne, a very famous French actor. He plays the typical Frenchman who enjoys life, jokes, friendship, and he never stops protesting.

Reference
Geography
Climate

The climate of France

The dividing lines between the climatic regions shown on the map are only approximate. There are wide areas where different regions overlap and merge into one another. Within each region in addition some variation in the climate may be produced by differences in relief or exposure. For instance, there is a marked contrast in climate between the coast and interior of Brittany.

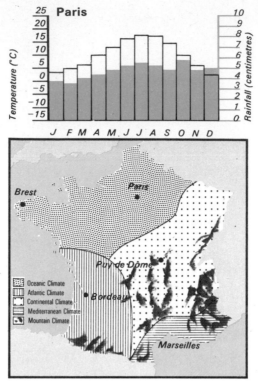

Oceanic Climate
Atlantic Climate
Continental Climate
Mediterranean Climate
Mountain Climate

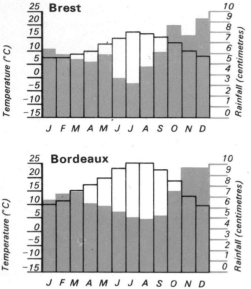

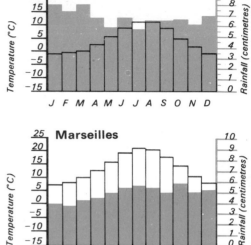

The dimensions of France

France is the largest country in Western Europe. With an area of 212,919 sq. miles, it is more than twice the size of the United Kingdom (though its population is smaller). The land area of France is also very compact, as the diagram below shows. From north to south and from east to west the longest distance is no more than 600 miles, and any line across the country from border to border measures about 600-650 miles. Also, no part of France is more than 250 miles from the sea. France is in fact more like a peninsula—the coast-line stretches for 1,760 miles while the land-frontiers measure only 1,665 miles.

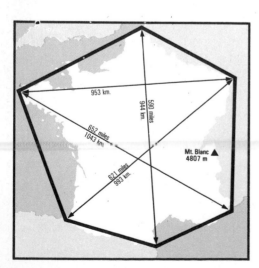

The natural vegetation of France

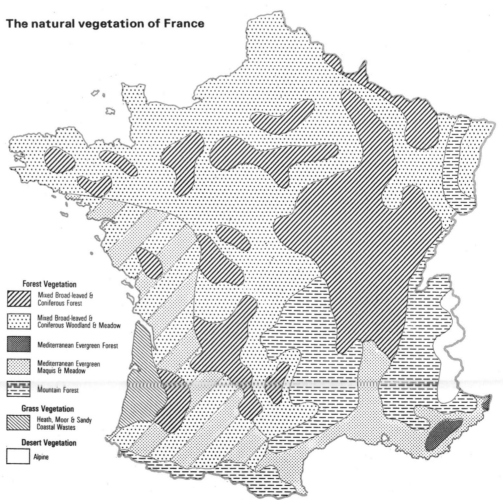

Forest Vegetation

Mixed Broad-leaved & Coniferous Forest

Mixed Broad-leaved & Coniferous Woodland & Meadow

Mediterranean Evergreen Forest

Mediterranean Evergreen Maquis & Meadow

Mountain Forest

Grass Vegetation

Heath, Moor & Sandy Coastal Wastes

Desert Vegetation

Alpine

The population density

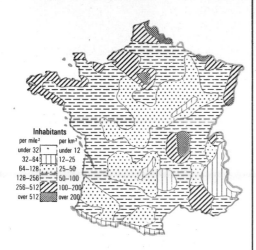

Inhabitants

per mile²		per km²
under 32		under 12
32–64		12–25
64–128		25–50
128–256		50–100
256–512		100–200
over 512		over 200

France is much less urbanized than West Germany or the United Kingdom because agriculture still plays a big part in the economy. The French population of 51 m. is smaller than Britain's even though France's area is over twice as big. The average density of population in France is therefore low. The population has been kept down by fairly high death and infant mortality rates earlier in the century. Immigration (Italians and Poles earlier, Algerians, Spaniards and Portuguese now) has helped to raise the numbers. Paris dwarfs all the other cities, especially in the north. Until recently it was the only conurbation with over 1 m. people.

The populations of principal towns

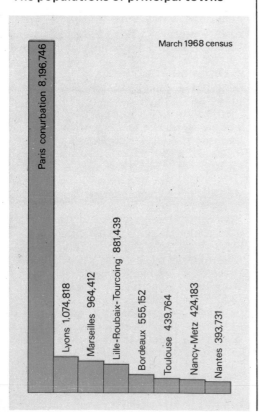

March 1968 census

Paris conurbation 8,196,746

Lyons 1,074,818

Marseilles 964,412

Lille-Roubaix-Tourcoing 881,439

Bordeaux 555,152

Toulouse 439,764

Nancy-Metz 424,183

Nantes 393,731

Administration

The Constitutional Structure

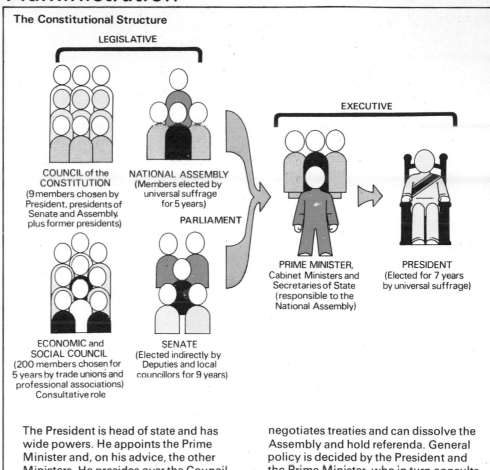

LEGISLATIVE

EXECUTIVE

COUNCIL of the CONSTITUTION (9 members chosen by President, presidents of Senate and Assembly, plus former presidents)

NATIONAL ASSEMBLY (Members elected by universal suffrage for 5 years)

PARLIAMENT

ECONOMIC and SOCIAL COUNCIL (200 members chosen for 5 years by trade unions and professional associations) Consultative role

SENATE (Elected indirectly by Deputies and local councillors for 9 years)

PRIME MINISTER, Cabinet Ministers and Secretaries of State (responsible to the National Assembly)

PRESIDENT (Elected for 7 years by universal suffrage)

The President is head of state and has wide powers. He appoints the Prime Minister and, on his advice, the other Ministers. He presides over the Council of Ministers, promulgates laws, negotiates treaties and can dissolve the Assembly and hold referenda. General policy is decided by the President and the Prime Minister, who in turn consults the other Ministers.

The local government structure

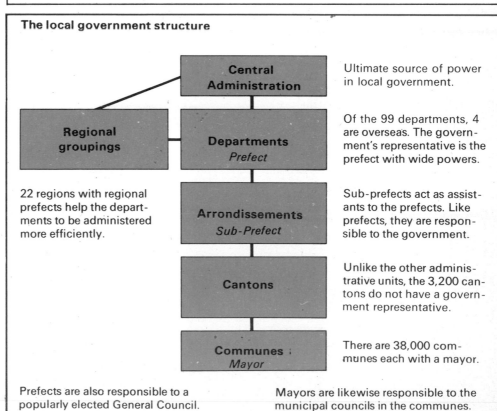

Central Administration — Ultimate source of power in local government.

Regional groupings

Departments *Prefect* — Of the 99 departments, 4 are overseas. The government's representative is the prefect with wide powers.

22 regions with regional prefects help the departments to be administered more efficiently.

Arrondissements *Sub-Prefect* — Sub-prefects act as assistants to the prefects. Like prefects, they are responsible to the government.

Cantons — Unlike the other administrative units, the 3,200 cantons do not have a government representative.

Communes *Mayor* — There are 38,000 communes each with a mayor.

Prefects are also responsible to a popularly elected General Council.

Mayors are likewise responsible to the municipal councils in the communes.

Reference
History

Main Events in French History

c.600 B.C.	Marseilles founded by Greeks
500	Celts invade Gaul
59-52	Caesar conquers Gaul
A.D. 250	Martyrdom of St. Denis
257	Invasion of Franks and Alamanni
451	Gallo-Romans defeat Attila's Huns
507	Clovis defeats Visigoths
732	Charles Martel checks Arabs at Poitiers
800	Charlemagne Holy Roman Emperor
911	Duchy of Normandy founded
1066	Normans conquer England
1095	Crusades launched at Clermont
1152	France loses Aquitaine to England
1204	England loses Normandy, Anjou, etc.
1337-1453	Hundred Years' War
1562-1598	Religious wars: Catholics v. Huguenots
1598	Edict of Nantes: Huguenots tolerated
1624-1642	Cardinal Richelieu virtual ruler
1648-1653	The Fronde rebellions of the nobility
1685	Edict of Nantes revoked
1756-1763	Seven Years' War: French lose colonies
1778-1783	French help American revolutionaries
1789-1815	French Revolution and Empire
1830	July revolution deposes Charles X
1848	Louis Philippe deposed; Louis Napoleon President of Second Republic
1852	Second Empire under Napoleon III
1854-1856	War against Russia in Crimea
1870	Prussian war: Napoleon III abdicates
1871	France defeated; Alsace and Lorraine lost; Thiers puts down Paris Commune, killing 20,000
1894-1906	Dreyfus affair
1914-1918	First World War
1919	Alsace and Lorraine returned
1939-1945	Second World War
1954	French lose Indo-China
1957	France joins Common Market
1958	Revolt of Algerian settlers brings De Gaulle back to power: Fifth Republic
1962	Algeria independent after 8-year war
1968	Revolt of students and workers
1969	De Gaulle loses referendum; resigns
1974	Death of President Pompidou; Giscard d'Estaing becomes President

56

How France grew through the ages

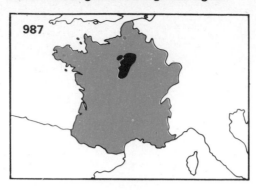
987

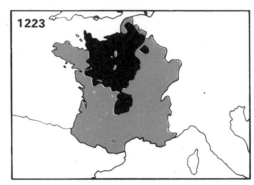
1223

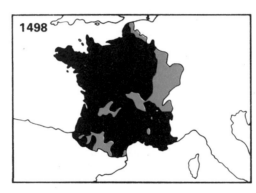
1498

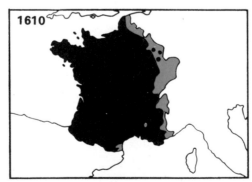
1610

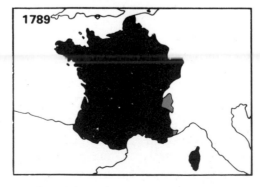
1789

KINGS
Merovingians   481-751

481- 511	Clovis

Carolingians   751-987

747- 768	Pepin the Short
771- 814	Charlemagne

Capetians   987-1328

987- 996	Hugh Capet
996-1031	Robert II, the Pious
1031-1060	Henry I
1060-1108	Philip I
1108-1137	Louis VI, the Fat
1137-1180	Louis VII, the Young
1180-1223	Philip II, Augustus
1223-1226	Louis VIII
1226-1270	Louis IX, St. Louis
1270-1285	Philip III
1285-1314	Philip IV, the Fair
1314-1316	Louis X
1316	John I
1316-1322	Philip V
1322-1328	Charles IV, the Fair

Valois   1328-1589

1328-1350	Philip VI
1350-1364	John II, the Good
1364-1380	Charles V, the Good
1380-1422	Charles VI, the Well-Loved
1422-1461	Charles VII, the Victorious
1461-1483	Louis XI
1483-1498	Charles VIII
1498-1515	Louis XII
1515-1547	Francis I
1547-1559	Henry II
1559-1560	Francis II
1560-1574	Charles IX
1574-1589	Henry III

Bourbons   1589-1792

1589-1610	Henry IV
1610-1643	Louis XIII
1643-1715	Louis XIV
1715-1774	Louis XV
1774-1792	Louis XVI

First Republic   1792-1799
Consulate and First Empire (Napoleon) 1799-1814
Restoration   1814-1848

1814-1824	Louis XVIII
1824-1830	Charles X
1830-1848	Louis-Philippe

Second Republic and Empire (Louis Napoleon/Napoleon III) 1848-1870

PRESIDENTS
Third, Fourth and Fifth Republics 1870-

1871-1873	Adolphe Thiers
1873-1879	Marshal MacMahon
1879-1887	Jules Grévy
1887-1894	Sadi Carnot
1894-1895	Jean Casimir-Périer
1895-1899	Félix Faure
1899-1906	Emile Loubet
1906-1913	Armand Fallières
1913-1920	Raymond Poincaré
1920	Paul Deschanel
1920-1924	Alexandre Millerand
1924-1931	Gaston Doumergue
1931-1932	Paul Doumer
1932-1940	Albert Lebrun
1947-1954	Vincent Auriol
1954-1959	René Coty
1959-1969	General Charles de Gaulle
1969-74	Georges Pompidou
1974—	Valéry Giscard d'Estaing

The Hundred Years' War with England 1337-1453

1328	Edward III of England claims French throne
1337	War begins; English hold Aquitaine
1346	Crécy: French defeated
1347	English take Calais
1356	English beat John II at Poitiers
1358	Peasant rising put down
1360	Peace of Brétigny
1369-80	Charles V frees most of country
1392	Charles VI goes mad: nobles disagree
1407	Civil war between Armagnacs and Burgundians
1415	Agincourt: French beaten again by English
1420	Troyes peace gives half France to England
1429	Joan of Arc raises English siege of Orléans, gets Charles VII crowned at Reims
1431	Joan burned at stake in Rouen
1453	English finally driven out (except Calais)

French Revolution and Empire 1789-1815

1789	Revolt at Rennes; bread riots (July 14) Fall of Bastille (Aug.) Feudal rights abolished (Nov.) Church lands taken over
1791	Flight of King Louis XVI to Varennes Legislative Assembly meets
1792	(Aug.) Attack on Tuileries; Assembly ends (Sept.) Convention meets; monarchy abolished; new calendar
1793	(Jan.) Execution of Louis XVI France at war with Britain, Spain, etc. Royalist revolt in the Vendée Committee of Public Safety set up Marat assassinated; Robespierre joins Committee; the Terror begins
1794	Foreign invasion warded off (July) 9 thermidor: Robespierre's fall
1795	Convention dissolved; Directory begins
1796-7	Napoleon's victories in Italy
1799	2nd Coalition of powers against France Napoleon returns from Egypt; coup d'état of 18 brumaire; Napoleon First Consul
1804	Napoleon Emperor
1805	Trafalgar: French fleet destroyed Austerlitz: Russia and Austria beaten
1807	Tilsit: Napoleon dictates to Russians
1812	French occupy, then retreat from Moscow
1814	Abdication of Napoleon; Louis XVIII back
1815	Napoleon returns; defeated at Waterloo; Louis XVIII restored again

Second World War 1939-45: the Germans invade

1939	(Sept.) Germany invades Poland; France and Britain declare war on Germany
1940	(May) French front broken on Meuse (June) Germans enter Paris; Pétain heads government; De Gaulle in London calls for resistance; French armistices with Germany and Italy— France divided into Nazi occupied and unoccupied (Vichy) zones
1941	German invasion of U.S.S.R.; French communists join and boost resistance
1942	Germans move into Vichy France; French fleet sinks itself at Toulon
1943	De Gaulle heads Free French at Algiers
1944	(June) Allied landing in Normandy (Aug.) De Gaulle enters Paris
1945	Constituent Assembly elected

May 1968: on the brink of revolution

2-11	Nanterre and Sorbonne (Paris) universities closed; student/police battles
12	General strike in support of students
14-16	Universities and factories occupied
21	Now 8 million on strike and 150 factories seized by workers; France at standstill
22	Assembly vote of censure on government fails
24	De Gaulle promises reform; pitched battles between police and students and workers
26-27	Tentative agreement between government, employers and trade unions on pay, etc.
30	De Gaulle warns of Communist threat and prepares for general elections; ½ million Gaullists march in Paris
31	Pompidou forms new cabinet

Writers, artists and composers

LITERATURE

La Chanson de Roland (c. 1100): epic poem
Rabelais (1490-1553): *Pantagruel, Gargantua*
Ronsard (1524-84): *Odes, Amours* (poems)
Montaigne (1533-92): *Essais*
Descartes (1596-1650): philosophy
Corneille (1606-84): *Le Cid* and other plays
La Fontaine (1621-95): *Les Fables*
Molière (1622-73): *Le Misanthrope,* other plays
Racine (1639-99): *Andromaque, Phèdre* (plays)
Montesquieu (1684-1755): novels, philosophy
Voltaire (1694-1778): *Lettres Philosophiques, Candide,* and all kinds of writing
Rousseau (1712-78)- *Le Contrat Social* (philosophy), *Emile* (education), *Confessions*
Diderot (1713-84): main author of *Encyclopédie*
Chateaubriand (1768-1848): early romantic
Stendhal (1783-1842): *Le Rouge et le Noir* (novel)
Balzac (1799-1850): *La Comédie Humaine*
Hugo (1802-85): *Notre-Dame-de-Paris, Les Misérables* (novels)
Flaubert (1821-80): *Madame Bovary* (novel)
Zola (1840-1902): *Germinal* (novel)
Gide (1869-1951): *La Porte Etroite,* other novels
Valéry (1871-1945): poet and philosopher
Proust (1871-1922): *A la recherche du temps perdu* (seven-part novel)
Sartre (1905-): novels, philosophy, plays
Camus (1913-60): *L'Etranger, La Peste, La Chute*

ART

Poussin (1594-1665): classicist; *Les Saisons*
Watteau (1684-1721): "genre" painter; *L'Indifférent*
David (1748-1825): classicist
Delacroix (1798-1863): romantic; *La Liberté*
Degas (1834-1917): impressionist
Cézanne (1839-1906): paved way for fauvists
Rodin (1840-1917): sculptor; *Le Penseur*
Monet (1840-1926): first major impressionist
Renoir (1841-1919): impressionist
Gauguin (1848-1903): used symbolism
Matisse (1869-1954): perhaps most important 20C. French artist and sculptor; fauvist
Dufy (1877-1953): fauvist
Braque (1882-1963): used wood, paper on paintings

MUSIC

Lully (1632-87): operas, ballets, overtures
Couperin (1668-1733): 200 harpsichord pieces
Rameau (1683-1764): operas, ballets
Berlioz (1803-69): symphonies, operas (*The Trojans*), choral works (*Damnation of Faust)*
Saint-Saëns (1835-1921): symphonies, concertos
Bizet (1838-75): operas (*Carmen*)
Debussy (1862-1918): impressionist influence; piano music, opera (*Pelléas et Melisande*)
Ravel (1875-1937): orchestral, piano works
Les Six: Poulenc, Milhaud, Honegger best known
Messiaen (1908-): greatest living composer

Reference
The Economy

Agriculture in France

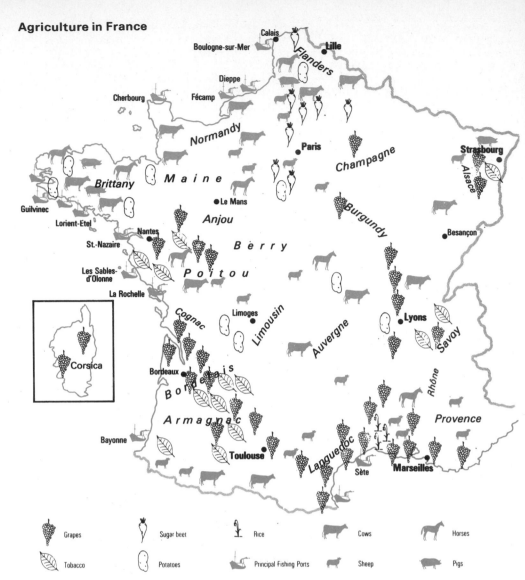

Grapes
Sugar beet
Rice
Cows
Horses
Tobacco
Potatoes
Principal Fishing Ports
Sheep
Pigs

Industrial growth

France is still the leading agricultural country in Europe: 60% of its land is cultivated, and it produces more cereals, milk, meat and sugar than West Germany, Italy or Britain.

But industry is being built up fast under the sixth 1971-75 plan. (France was the first state after the U.S.S.R. to introduce economic planning, and many major industries like cars and aviation are state-run.) Industry grew fast after 1958 when France went into the European Common Market (E.E.C.). French industrialists were forced to modernize and expand to compete with the Germans when the protective barriers were removed. They were helped by France's varied resources and by their willingness to learn new management techniques. The Mirage jet-fighters, the (Anglo-French) Concorde and Citroën and Renault cars are now as well respected abroad as Bordeaux and Burgundy wines.

Despite a series of wars and crises (in 1968 the economy stopped working for almost six weeks) the French economy is growing faster than any other industrial nation except Japan and the U.S.S.R. If present trends continue, by 1980 the Frenchman's average income will be twice as much as the Briton's. By 1985 the French standard of living will be as high as Sweden's.

Industrial growth has been rapid since 1969 when the franc was devalued by 12·5 per cent. This meant that French exports became cheaper to foreign buyers and imports into France more expensive. The advantage was made greater by the fact that the true value of the franc in gold was slightly more than the value the French government fixed.

Exports have thus played an important part in France's growth. The trade balance (the amount by which export earnings exceed import costs) has been steadily improving. More than half of French sales abroad are now manufactures, and cars are an important part of these. The mainstay of exports is still farm goods (20% of the total). More than two-thirds of these are sold to E.E.C. countries, where the Common Agricultural Policy guarantees artificially high prices. Over half of all French trade is now with the E.E.C.; less than 10% with its former colonies.

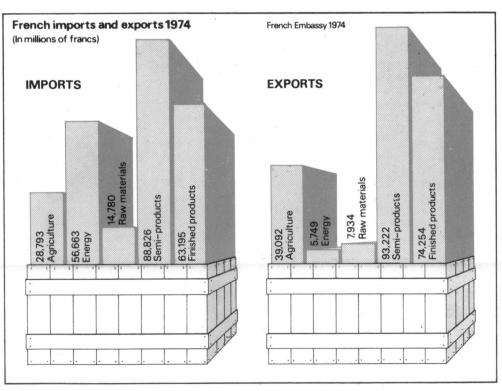

French imports and exports 1974
(In millions of francs)

French Embassy 1974

IMPORTS

28,793 Agriculture
56,663 Energy
14,780 Raw materials
88,826 Semi-products
63,195 Finished products

EXPORTS

39,092 Agriculture
5,749 Energy
7,934 Raw materials
93,222 Semi-products
74,254 Finished products

How labour is employed

O.E.C.D. 1973

Population in paid employment 20,953,000 of which:

(Total population 52,177,000)

12·2% are engaged in agriculture

39·3% are engaged in industry

48·5% are engaged in other occupations

Agriculture produces less national wealth per person employed than industry because working the land is by its nature less mechanized and produces less valuable goods.

Industry in France

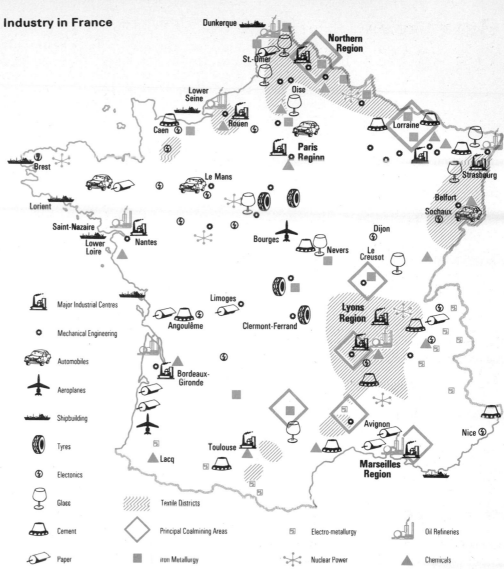

Dunkerque

Northern Region

St.-Omer

Oise

Lower Seine

Caen

Rouen

Paris Region

Lorraine

Strasbourg

Brest

Le Mans

Belfort

Sochaux

Lorient

Dijon

Saint-Nazaire

Nantes

Bourges

Nevers

Le Creusot

Lower Loire

Limoges

Lyons Region

Angoulême

Clermont-Ferrand

Bordeaux-Gironde

Avignon

Nice

Toulouse

Lacq

Marseilles Region

Major Industrial Centres

Mechanical Engineering

Automobiles

Aeroplanes

Shipbuilding

Tyres

Electonics

Glass

Cement

Paper

Textile Districts

Principal Coalmining Areas

Iron Metallurgy

Electro-metallurgy

Nuclear Power

Oil Refineries

Chemicals

What is owned compared to other countries

Though France compares well with other advanced countries in the numbers of consumer goods its people can afford to buy, it lags behind on more basic things like housing, which the government has neglected. Wealth is also very unevenly spread: the rich are very rich and the poor very poor.

Units per 1000 inhabitants
OECD 1971-72

237 France
293 Germany
202 Italy
225 Japan
305 Great Britain
474 U.S.A.

260 France
239 Germany
209 Italy
100 Japan
219 Great Britain
443 U.S.A.

199 France
268 Germany
206 Italy
315 Japan
314 Great Britain
628 U.S.A.

The rise in prices and incomes

in percentage increase

160
150
140
130
120
110
100

Hourly wages

Prices

1968   1969   1970   1971   1972

Inflation is a big problem in France, as elsewhere. Prices continue to rise sharply, mainly because of world rises in costs of food. This has pushed up wages, as has the shortage of skilled labour and trade union pressure.

Gazetteer

Alps. 46 to 47 0N 6 to 10 0E. Principal mountains in Europe covering 100,000 sq. m. Drained by Rhône in France.

Alsace. 48 30N 7 30E. Region in the north-east between the Vosges and Rhine. For long part of Germany and again (with Lorraine) 1871-1919. Chief towns Strasbourg, Mulhouse.

Anjou. 47 20N 0 50W. Former province. Capital Angers. Anjou was under the English Crown in the 12th and 13th centuries.

Blanc, Mont. 45 52N 6 50E. Highest mountain (15,781 ft.) in Alps. Several sharp peaks (aiguilles). First climbed 1786.

Bordeaux. 44 45N 0 38W. Prefecture of Gironde dept. on Garonne river. Chief port and commercial centre of south-west France. Wines famous. Pop. 555,000.

Brittany. 48 0N 2 10W. Caesar's Armorica. Former duchy and province. Settled by Celtic refugees from Britain in 5th century A.D. Noted for seafaring, ancient monuments and folklore.

Burgundy. 47 0N 4 50E. Former province. Famous for wines. Settled in 5th century A.D. by Germanic Burgundii tribe.

Caen. 49 15N 0 27W. Port and industrial, commercial and university centre in Normandy. Principal seat of William the Conqueror. City centre destroyed 1944. Pop. 114,398.

Cannes. 43 35N 0 0E. Principal resort of Riviera, 16m. south-west of Nice. Lord Brougham began its development as a resort in 1834. Pop. 213,000.

Champagne. 49 0N 4 30E. District and former province. Famous wines are produced on slopes between Reims and Epernay.

Corsica. 42 0N 9 0E. Island north of Sardinia in Mediterranean. Area 3,367 sq. m. Pop. 269,831. Department of France though more akin to Italy. Napoleon born at Ajaccio. Long tradition of banditry and vendettas.

Gascony. 43 40N 0 10E. Former province between Bay of Biscay and Pyrenees. Under English crown 1154-1453.

Grenoble. 45 12N 5 44E. Prefecture of Isère dept. and chief tourist centre of French Alps. Famous for kid-gloves; now also engineering and metallurgical industries. Ancient fortified city with cathedral (11th/13th centuries) and famous university (1339). Pop. 332,000.

Le Havre. 49 32N 0 5E. Important port at mouth of Seine on English Channel. Industries: oil-refining (pipeline to Paris), machinery, chemicals, flour-milling. Badly damaged in 2nd World War. Pop. 247,000.

Jura. 46 40N 6 5E. Mountains along border with Switzerland. Highest point 5,653 ft.

Languedoc. 43 50N 3 30E. Region and former province in south. *Langue d'oc* is Provençal: *oc*='yes' in southern France.

Lens. 50 27N 2 49E. Coal-mining centre near Lille. Badly damaged in both World Wars. Pop. 325,000.

Lille. 50 38N 3 0E. Prefecture of Nord dept. Great commercial and industrial centre. Fourth largest French city. Industries: textiles, chemicals, engineering, metallurgy, brewing. Flemish influence. Birthplace of de Gaulle. Pop. 881,000.

Loire. 47 40N 2 30E. Longest (627m.) river, flowing from Massif Central through Vichy, Orléans and Nantes to Bay of Biscay. With its tributaries, drains over fifth of France.

Lorraine. 48 58N 6 0E. Region and former province in east containing Meuse and Moselle valleys. Part of it, with Alsace, was incorporated into Germany 1871-1919.

Lyons. 45 47N 4 50E. Second largest city in France. Capital of Rhône dept. at confluence of Rhône and Saône rivers. Textile centre since 15th century, especially silks. Also financial centre. Founded by Romans 43 B.C. Strong revolutionary tradition after 1793. Centre of resistance movement in 2nd World War. Pop. 1,074,000.

Marseilles. 43 21N 5 22E. France's third city and principal port, on south coast 25m. east of Rhône delta. Originally founded c. 600 B.C. Large trade with North Africa and Asia. Industries: ships, chemicals, soap, oil-refining. Pop. 964,000

Massif Central. 44 50N 30E. Mountains dominating southern half of France. Highest points volcanic, eg. Mt. Dore (6,188 ft.) in Auvergne.

Médoc. 45 15N 1 0W. District in Gironde dept. in south-west. Occupies strip on left bank of Gironde estuary. Famous for clarets.

Nancy. 48 44N 6 10E. Prefecture of Meurthe-et-Moselle dept. and former capital of Lorraine. Iron and steel centre. Pop. 257,000.

Nantes. 47 17N 1 34W. Prefecture of Loire-Atlantique dept. on Loire estuary rivalling Rennes as chief town of Brittany. Important seaport with outport at St. Nazaire. Industries: ships, oil-refining, flour-milling. Edict of Nantes (1598) gave religious freedom to Huguenots. Pop. 393,000.

Nice. 43 45N 7 17E. Fashionable Riviera resort. Also textiles, paper, vegetable oil industries. Founded c.3rd century B.C. Birthplace of Garibaldi. Pop. 392,000.

Normandy. 49 0N 0 0. Region and former province in north-west. Norsemen founded duchy in tenth century. Battlefield in Second World War. Much dairy farming (e.g. Camembert cheese) and wheat. Capital Rouen. Ports: Le Havre, Cherbourg, Dieppe. Also Caen, etc.

Paris. 48 52N 2 18E. Capital of France and dept. on rivers Seine and Marne. By far the largest city (8.2m.) with sixth of total population. Centre of French communications and important European centre. Leading inland port. Seine crossed by 33 bridges. Centre of luxury industries, e.g. jewellery, cosmetics. and of tourism. Car and aircraft industries located in suburbs.

Named after Celtic tribe, Parisii. Abounds in historic buildings and monuments. Sorbonne (1150) one of oldest universities in world. Modern city laid out with wide boulevards by Baron Haussmann after 1855.

Picardy. 49 50N 3 0E. Region and former province in north. Capital Amiens, centre of textile industry. Saw heavy fighting in First World War.

Provence. 43 55N 6 10E. Former province on Mediterranean coast. Home of Provençal language. Independent kingdom until 1486.

Pyrénées. 42 30N 1 0E. Mountain range separating France and Spain. French side noted for mountain torrents and spas and resorts.

Reims. 49 18N 40E. Centre of champagne industry in Marne dept. Magnificent 13th century cathedral (restored 1938). German surrender signed here May 1945. Pop. 158,634.

Rennes. 48 10N 1 41W. Cultural centre and former capital of Britanny. Badly damaged in great fire 1720 and 2nd World War. Pop. 188,515.

Rhône. 45 58N 4 35E. One of chief European rivers. Rises in Switzerland, flowing west to Lyons, then south to Mediterranean. With its most important tributary, the Saône, it has been the major line of communication between the north and south of France for centuries.

Rouen. 49 28N 1 7E. Former capital of Normandy. Old quarter of 'the Gothic city' largely destroyed in 2nd World War. William the Conqueror died and Joan of Arc burned here. Pop, 124,577

St. Étienne. 43 12N 1 30W. On second largest coalfield in France. Iron, steel and silk produced. Pop. 331,000.

Seine. 48 57N 2 25E. Third longest river but first in economic importance. Rises 18m. north-west of Dijon; meanders through Paris and on to English Channel. Canals link it to the Meuse, Rhône, Loire, Rhine and Scheldt. 482m. long.

Strasbourg. 48 35N 7 46E. Principal inland port on Rhine and Ill rivers. Business and cultural centre of Alsace. Notable cathedral. European Parliament normally meets in Strasbourg. Pop. 334,000.

Toulon. 43 9N 5 55E. Important naval base with related industries on Mediterranean. French fleet scuttled itself here 1942 to prevent German seizure. Pop. 340,000.

Toulouse. 43 37N 1 18E. Former capital of Languedoc between Pyrenees and Massif Central. 2nd oldest university (1230). Pop. 439,000.

Tours. 47 24N 0 41E. Prefecture of Indre-et-Loire dept. and manufacturing and tourist centre. Near here Charles Martel won historic victory over Moors in 732. Pop. 132,861.

Valenciennes. 50 20N 3 32E. Coal-mining and industrial town in Nord dept. near Lille on river Escaut (Scheldt). Pop. 223,000.

Vosges. 48 20N 7 0E. Mountains near Franco-German border resembling Black Forest on opposite (German) side of Rhine. Highest point 4,665 ft.

Index

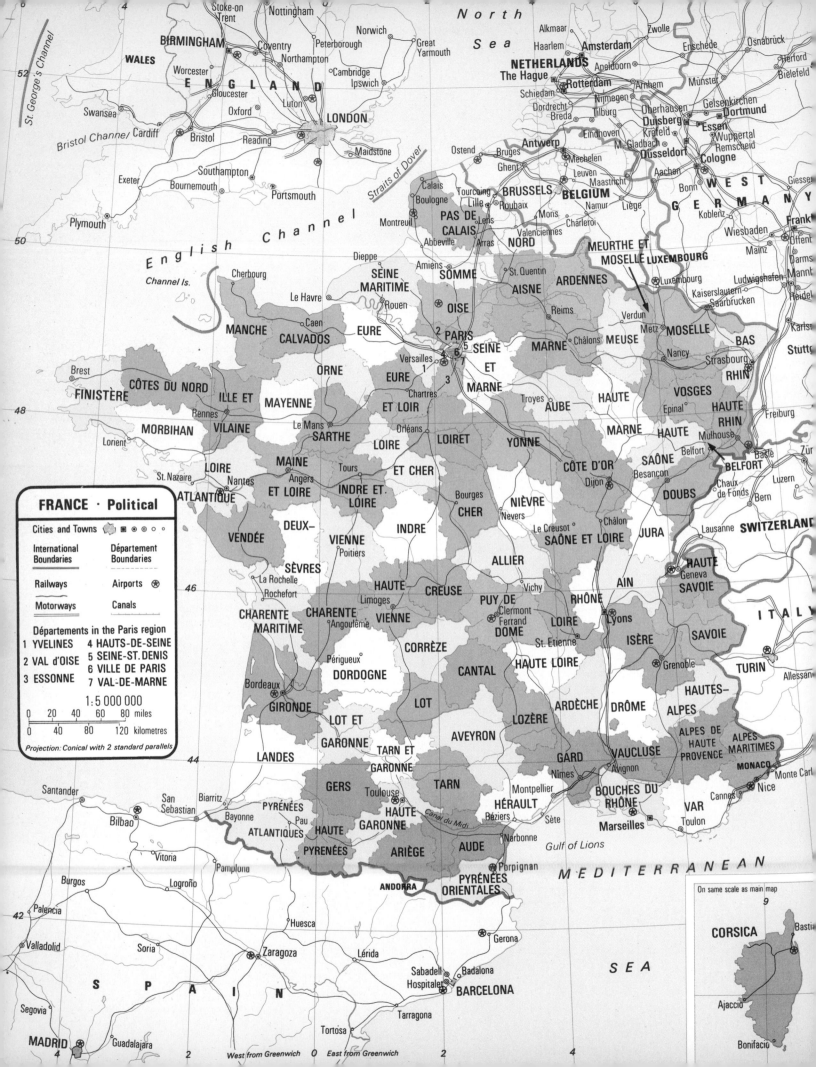

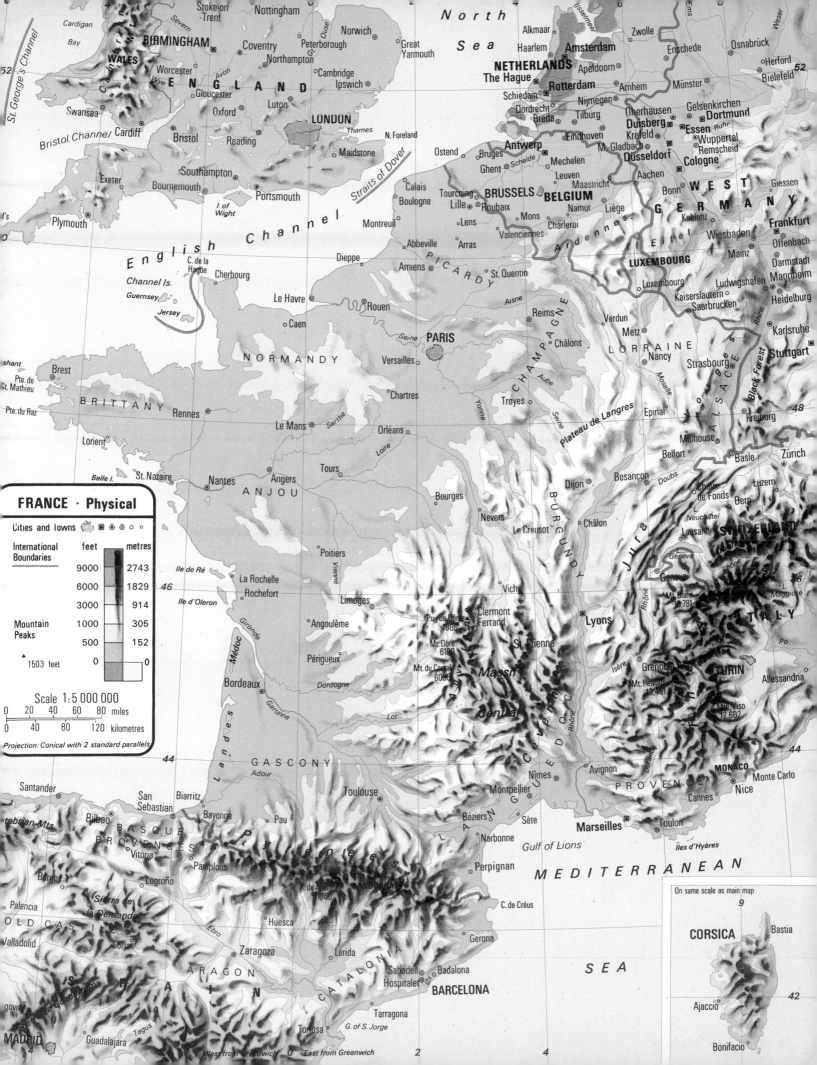

FRANCE · Physical

Cities and towns

International Boundaries

feet	metres
9000	2743
6000	1829
3000	914
1000	305
500	152
0	0

Mountain Peaks

▲ 1503 feet

Scale 1:5 000 000

0 20 40 60 80 miles
0 40 80 120 kilometres

Projection: Conical with 2 standard parallels

Map labels

North Sea
St. George's Channel
Cardigan Bay
Stoke-on-Trent
Nottingham
Norwich
Alkmaar
Zwolle
Osnabrück
BIRMINGHAM
Coventry
Peterborough
Northampton
Great Yarmouth
Amsterdam
Haarlem
Enschede
Herford
Bielefeld
WALES
Worcester
Cambridge
Ipswich
NETHERLANDS
Apeldoorn
Münster
52
Swansea
ENGLAND
Gloucester
Wye
Oxford
Luton
The Hague
Rotterdam
Arnhem
Nijmegen
Oberhausen
Gelsenkirchen
Dortmund
Bristol Channel
Cardiff
Bristol
Reading
LONDON
Schiedam
Dordrecht
Tilburg
Duisberg
Essen
Ruhr
Wuppertal
Remscheid
Cologne
Bournemouth
Southampton
Portsmouth
Maidstone
N. Foreland
Breda
Eindhoven
M. Gladbach
Düsseldorf
Krefeld
Aachen
WEST
Exeter
I. of Wight
Straits of Dover
Ostend
Bruges
Antwerp
Mechelen
Maastricht
Bonn
GERMANY
Giessen
Plymouth
Calais
Boulogne
Tourcoing
Lille
Roubaix
BRUSSELS
BELGIUM
Leuven
Liège
Ardennes
Eifel
Wiesbaden
Frankfurt
English Channel
C. de la Hague
Cherbourg
Montreuil
Arras
Lens
Mons
Charleroi
Namur
LUXEMBOURG
Koblenz
Offenbach
Mainz
Darmstadt
Mannheim
Channel Is.
Guernsey
Jersey
Dieppe
Abbeville
Amiens
PICARDY
St. Quentin
Valenciennes
Luxembourg
Verdun
Kaiserslautern
Saarbrucken
Ludwigshafen
Heidelburg
shant
Pte. de St. Mathieu
Brest
Le Havre
Rouen
Aisne
Reims
Châlons
Metz
Nancy
LORRAINE
Moselle
Strasbourg
Karlsruhe
Stuttgart
Pte. du Raz
BRITTANY
Rennes
Caen
NORMANDY
Seine
PARIS
Versailles
CHAMPAGNE
Aube
Epinal
ALSACE
Black Forest
48
Lorient
Le Mans
Sarthe
Chartres
Troyes
Yonne
Seine
Plateau de Langres
Freiburg
St. Nazaire
Belle I.
Nantes
Angers
ANJOU
Tours
Orléans
Loire
Bourges
Nevers
Dijon
Doubs
Besancon
BURGUNDY
Jura
Mulhouse
Belfort
Basle
Zurich
Chaux-de-Fonds
Bern
Neuchâtel
Luzern
SWITZERLAND
Lausanne
Geneva
Ile de Ré
Poitiers
Vienne
Vichy
Châlon
Le Creusot
Geneva
Rhône
46
La Rochelle
Rochefort
Ile d'Oléron
Limoges
Angoulême
Puy de Dôme
4805
Clermont Ferrand
St. Etienne
Lyons
Grenoble
Mt. Blanc
12,781
ITALY
Lago Maggiore
Médoc
Périgueux
Mt. Dore
6188
Massif
Isère
TURIN
Gironde
Bordeaux
Dordogne
Mt. du Cantal
6096
Central
Rhône
Mt. Pelvoux
12,461
Allessandria
Lot
Durance
Mte. Viso
12,602
Po
44
Garonne
GASCONY
Adour
Avignon
Nîmes
MONACO
Monte Carlo
Santander
San Sebastian
Biarritz
Bayonne
Pau
Toulouse
Montpellier
PROVENCE
Cannes
Nice
Bilbao
Vitoria
BASQUE PROVINCES
Béziers
Sète
Narbonne
Toulon
Cantabrian Mts.
Pyrenees
Marseilles
goviu
Burgos
Pamplona
Gulf of Lions
Îles d'Hyères
Sierra de la Demanda
Logroño
Huesca
Perpignan
MEDITERRANEAN
OLD CASTILE
Ebro
Zaragoza
Lérida
Gerona
C. de Créus
Palencia
ARAGON
CATALONIA
Sabadell
Badalona
SEA
Valladolid
Soria
Tagus
Guadalajara
MADRID
Tortosa
G. of S. Jorge
Tarragona
Huesca
Hospitalet
BARCELONA
West from Greenwich
East from Greenwich

CORSICA (inset — *On same scale as main map*)
Bastia
Ajaccio
Bonifacio
42